PLATFORM SOULS

Nicholas Whittaker began trainspotting during the height of Beatlemania. Now a journalist, he has written for a wide range of publications, from *Company* to the *Sunday Times*, and lives with his family in north London. He no longer collects train numbers, but still displays Pavlovian impulses by reaching for a biro whenever he catches a whiff of diesel fuel.

NICHOLAS WHITTAKER

PLATFORM SOULS

The Trainspotter as
Twentieth-Century Hero

CASSELL PLC

INDIGO

First published in Great Britain 1995
by Victor Gollancz

This Indigo edition published 1996
Indigo is an imprint of the Cassell Group
Wellington House, 125 Strand, London WC2R 0BB

© Nicholas Whittaker 1995

The right of Nicholas Whittaker to be identified as author
of this work has been asserted by him in accordance with
the Copyright, Designs and Patents Act, 1988.

A catalogue record for this book is
available from the British Library.

ISBN 0 575 40011 0

Printed and bound in Great Britain by
Guernsey Press Co. Ltd,
Guernsey, Channel Isles

96 97 98 99   10 9 8 7 6 5 4 3 2 1

For my Mum, with thanks for all the pocket money and the well-packed sandwiches, and for Martin, Oliver and Robin in the hope they'll have as much fun as I had . . .

Acknowledgements: My thanks to Liz Knights and Mike Petty and everyone at Gollancz who liked the idea, and especially Ian Preece for all his editorial guidance and moral support (and the chicken Madras). Not forgetting all my trainspotting pals past and present, Andy's dad for taking us out and having the foresight to take a camera, and Alf Moss for digging deep into his archives to find that special picture.

Picture Acknowledgements: pages 19, 35, 37, 43, 47, 210: W. Parker; pages 27, 31, 215: R. C. Riley; pages 67, 117, 142, 219: Brian Morrison; pages 74, 170: Brian Stephenson; page 59: Alf Moss Collection; pages 10, 57, 84, 94, 140, 156, 173, 181, 194, 201, 227, 229, 249: Nicholas Whittaker

contents

Prologue: Birmingham New Street, 1995

Early Years

The Seventies

The Eighties

Today's Scene

Postscript: Burton-on-Trent, 1995

Prologue: Birmingham New Street, 1995

If there was an ugliest railway station competition, and I were one of the judges, I'd stick my neck out for Birmingham New Street. It's always been one of my least favourite places. I don't mind the dark cuttings with their tenacious ferns and furred sediment that's been trapped on the ledges since the steam age. Rather, it's the station itself that I hate. Low-ceilinged, harshly lit, square-cut, it's one of the real horrors of the sixties. We still have plenty of lovely stations – York, Bristol Temple Meads, St Pancras, Rugby – but Birmingham was built to be despised. Not only that, it's so drearily suburban. There are Class 90 electrics on the Euston shuttle trains and Flying Bananas on the Bristol–Newcastle route, but the rest is all local stuff, Sprinter units ferrying workers and shoppers to places like Aston and Walsall and Dudley.

Yet these are the moans of one man, obviously not shared by the scores of trainspotters who come here every weekend. Men like Alan Knowsley, amiable and balding, the left-hand pocket of his jacket so distorted by spotting books that it keeps its square shape even when he takes them out. As he looks around the gloomy concrete canyon at the top end of Platform 8, his face is lit by the slightly crazed smile of a psychic. While shoppers and students wait for the 11.45 to York, Alan can see ghost trains and hear the crackle of ancient loudspeaker announcements.

'Imagine, Jason, the exhaust on a Coronation taking one of the big expresses out.' Alan gazes towards the top floors of the looming rotunda, imagining a billowing column of engine smoke.

Jason, his son, looks puzzled. 'Big express' has a quaint ring to it now. He's heard of InterCity and Cross-Country, smart marketing concepts invented by men in

Just another spotting Saturday at Birmingham New Street

red specs and fancy braces, but big express? It sounds like something off kiddies' TV. He folds another Juicy Fruit between his teeth and tries to take it seriously for his dad's sake. But Alan's on to a loser. Not matter how many tales he thinks up, he'll never convince Jason there was a time when all a lad needed to be happy was a biro and notebook and a duffel bag with some Marmite sandwiches.

Trainspotting carries a heavy cargo of nostalgia, and there's nothing wrong with that. If it's good crack now, it was even better three decades ago. There were more trains, livelier stations, busier engine sheds. The country was a different place then.

In the fifties, Alan's army was a hundred thousand strong: *Just William* kids standing at the trackside to salute the trains and their drivers. This was England at its monochrome best: smoky and proud, sadly oblivious to the political skulduggery that was going to change it for ever. But those kids have long gone. Today's trainspotter – he'd prefer 'railfan' – is a grown-up with a credit card. He has made a Faustian pact with Dixons and comes fully equipped with camcorder, Pentax with auto-wind and telephoto, and a personal stereo on which to listen to Fleetwood Mac between trains.

Progress is inevitable, but there's been a more drastic change. The trainspotter has become everyone's favourite wally. With blacks, gays and big-boobed women all off the right-on comic's agenda, here's a man you can titter at in safety, political integrity unblemished. The Identikit is hideous: a gormless loner with dandruff and halitosis, a sad case obsessed by numbers, timetables and signalling procedures. He has no interest in girls, and girls have even less interest in him.

What on earth happened? No one used to take the piss. Trainspotting was our national hobby, as English as morris dancing and looked on with indulgence. We had the best trains in the world, it was only natural that kids took an interest.

Those comics have a lot to answer for. They've made a pariah out of a harmless eccentric and totally destroyed the market in anoraks – all for a cheap laugh. Yet no one has ever specified exactly what the problem is, or explained why trainspotting is any more futile than, say, golf, stamp collecting or keeping tropical fish. The character assassination has been so complete that to protest innocence is only to dig a deeper hole.

As society becomes more TV dependent and we enjoy everything by proxy – sport, crime, road accidents, even practical jokes – so we are encouraged to despise eccentricity. Daftness is for TV personalities, not for the likes of you and me. Once harmless hobbies are redefined as sad and definitely untrendy. And unselfconscious trainspotters, unaware they need an excuse for their interest, are sitting targets. I suspect that further scorn lavished on trainspotting is an inevitable side-effect of a culture obsessed by cars. Interest in any other form of transport is regarded as eccentric. Fast cars and posh cars are aspirational, but railways (and buses) are seen as a second-class form of travel, ergo any interest in them must be suspect and pitiable.

But how far will it go? In December 1994 a man found guilty of stealing rare bird eggs was described by the prosecution as a kind of 'railway spotter' – one more step in the demonization process, and a rather sinister one. It's one thing to make fun of a man for liking trains, but to use him as a stereotype for a criminal is surely dangerous. The trouble is, people have never forgotten that Michael Sams, the infamous kidnapper-murderer, was a quiet man whose hobby was trainspotting. He was even wearing his enamelled loco badges when he carried out his crimes. Such things sink into the collective sub-conscious, and stay there.

Years ago Birmingham had another big station: Snow Hill. With its Great Western colours and holiday posters, it whispered rumours to small trainspotters of places beyond their ken; places like Oxford and Paddington, Torquay and Weymouth. I first went there in the spring of 1965. My mum and nanna were off shopping in Birmingham, and instead of me whingeing all afternoon I suggested they dropped me off at Snow Hill and came back for me later. I'd heard about Snow Hill and was prepared to love it straight away; there was even a red carpet on the stairs down to the platform! What a welcome. The trainspotters' view was limited by a black tunnel mouth at either end, yet instead of being irritated, I was fascinated. The tunnels tightened the station's perspective and reminded me of the little doorway in *Alice in Wonderland*; when the train emerged on the far side there would be sunshine and open skies and a great sense of adventure.

But I find myself talking of the past too often. It's the present I'm seeking to understand.

*   *   *

'Look, Dad!' yells Jason, suddenly galvanized. 'There's *The Clothes Show*.' As the Class 90 electric slips out of the station with its Euston-bound train, Jason takes an interest. He's finally found something he can identify with.

Alan smiles bravely. The engines he remembers from the Golden Age had names like *Princess Elizabeth*, *Gold Coast*, *Pendennis Castle*, names which reflected the glories of royalty and Empire. Hardly PC, of course, but better than today's tributes to important customers: *Rugeley Power Station*, *Blue Circle Cement*, *The CBI*. *Britannia* and *Royal Scot* were names revered by all boys, majestic steamers that thundered past on North–South expresses. Still, electrics are better than nothing. Alan swings his camcorder towards the Class 90. Its driver gives a cheesy grin. With the number of home videos being made these days, it won't be long before someone sets up a make-up department for image-conscious ASLEF men.

But I can understand Alan's predicament: it's not just the engines that fascinate the trainspotter. He clings, like a burr to a tapestry, hooked and entangled in the whole fabric of the railways. He loves the addictive smell of diesel fuel, the signals that blink from red to green, the rattle of station announcements, the driver with his pipe, and the tortured squeak on the rails as a 'Brush' pulls 500 tons of carriages out of the station.

And then there's silence, one of those odd moments you get, even on the busiest station, when nothing moves and all the signals are at red. Jason chews gum and kicks a fag packet up and down the platform. Alan has time to think, and I can imagine him worrying about the future. The trainspotter is an endangered species; the railway magazines are full of obituaries these days, tributes to pals from the golden years at Paddington, Crewe and York:

> . . . the stained glass window in his
> local church, paid for by friends and

incorporating Ted on the footplate of
Pixie, will ensure that his memory
lives on . . .

Dads try their best to pass on the eccentric gene, but today's youngsters are more interested in trainers than trains. Trainspotting promises no excitement now. When a country despises its railways like we do, it's no surprise that our youngsters don't carry a torch for them. But it's not just the jokes that keep the kids away – there are no role models any more. Railwaymen used to be our heroes, gritty working-class men with denim overalls and jaunty caps. We couldn't wait to grow up and work alongside them. Who could aspire to be a railwayman today, squeaky clean in corporate uniform and parroting phrases from the *Customer Care Manual*?

Early Years

001 Steamer Gates, 1964

It was Adrian 'Bolt' Brown who introduced me to trainspotting in that first summer holiday after leaving Christ Church Junior Mixed & Infants. Considering I'd broken his arm only a few weeks before, during a game of Wagon Train in the school yard, it was a generous gesture. I was glad of his offer, since I felt in need of some distraction. Even at the age of eleven I was wise enough to guess that life would never be the same again. At secondary school there'd be no belting out 'Go And Tell Aunt Nancy', no squabbling for the privilege of fetching sir's mid-morning tea, no brassy clanging hand-bell to signal hometime.

There was another reason for sadness. I'd just got my first broken heart. A song called 'Juliet' by the Four Pennies was on the radio a lot that summer, and every time I heard it I wanted to cry. My love's name was actually Olga Jaworski, a brown-eyed pink-cardiganed girl I'd happily ignored for the past four years before suddenly getting all soppy about. But 'Juliet' was sad and perfect for the way I felt. We were going our separate ways now – me to the grammar school, Olga to the technical – and my little heart was all churned up.

Little did she or I know how quickly she would be brushed aside for the smoky charms of British Railways.

Trainspotting was as simple as it was brilliant, Bolt reckoned. All you needed was a biro and a sixpenny notebook from the paper shop; even a schoolkid could afford the kit. Then you just went along to 'Steamer Gates' and sat and watched the trains pass by. There were plenty of them, and enough variety to keep any curious child happy: thundering expresses with passengers' faces pressed to steamy windows; rattling freights packed with boxes and bottles; long, slow coal trains that left us choking in clouds of black grit.

I'd always been aware of the railways. Burton was criss-crossed with lines running between its dozens of breweries, maltings and loading bays. Dawdling home from school, I'd often be stopped in my tracks by white-painted crossing gates swinging out across the street and a clanging bell heralding a train. With no more urgent worries than nibbling the diddies off a liquorice pipe or stopping my Cornish Mivvi falling off its stick, I was happy to stop and watch. From somewhere, out of a world of men and work and brewing smells, a red Toy-town tank engine would come wheezing past with half a dozen wagons. The motorists tutted and looked at their watches, but I was as fascinated as any young boy would be. Then it was gone, the sight and sound of it swallowed up between the high walls and shadowed wharves. The motorists gave a collective sigh of relief, the gates wobbled open, and we all went on our way, the motorists about their business, me home for a tea of Stork and honey sandwiches.

It was all quite fascinating, but the idea of train-spotting had never crossed my mind until Bolt suggested it. I told him I liked watching Bass's tank engines, but he wasn't impressed. That was just kid's stuff, cutesy little puffers on an overgrown model railway. The serious business took place on the main Newcastle–Bristol line which ran through the town, just a few hundred yards from Christ Church Junior school. Trainspotting was second nature to the kids who lived in the back streets behind the school; they went to bed each night with the clangety-clangety-clang sound of shunting for a lullaby, and it must have worked its way into their subconscious.

I'd been through a few hobbies of late – car-spotting, fossil collecting, magnetism – but they were all lonely hobbies, show-off hobbies, only-child hobbies. In any case, there were no fossils in Burton; the Palaeozoic Age seemed to have missed the town altogether. Trainspotting was different; here was a real boy's hobby with its own gaberdine camaraderie. It was dirty and mechanical, proudly masculine and solid, yet at the same time (for me at least) romantic and educational. The railways might be a magic carpet that could take you anywhere.

Bolt probably expected me to slope off after an hour, but I was hooked. Perched precariously on top of the level crossing gates, and then sprawled on the embankment with an ice lolly, I knew straight away this would be the perfect way to spend that important summer.

There were rules to be learned and lore to absorb. For the first time with any of my hobbies, I couldn't swot

Summer-holiday moment. An 8-Freight on the High Level line at Lichfield Trent Valley, 1965

up from books. I had to just listen and watch and remember. I knew the difference between a steamer and a diesel, of course, but I could soon tell a Duck Six (Bolt: 'It's got an 0–6–0 wheel arrangement, see?') from a Jubilee ('It's a 4–6–0 and it's a namer'). The Jubilees sounded like fun, and I loved their exotic names – *Sierra Leone*, *Bechuanaland*, *Punjab* – but this was long before I grew up to despise the glorification of the Empire.

There were bound to be mistakes, but a chorus of

mockery from the other lads ensured that I'd never again jot down a destination headcode from the front of a diesel unit, or feverishly try to record the numbers of all the carriages as they rushed by. Before the end of the day I was even joining in the loud chorus of 'Scrap it!' that greeted any engine we'd already seen once. Bolt was a bit more daring; instead of the childish 'Scrap it!' he had a new arsenal of swearwords. 'You old bleeder!' he shouted gleefully at 8-Freights and Ozzies he'd already got the number of. The drivers glared back at him – if they had been motorists they'd probably have stopped to give him a smack around the head. I was too well brought up to use such language, but I thought it brilliantly daring.

I wasn't prepared for the ecstatic display which greeted one particular engine. Yes, it was green and well-polished, but why was everyone going mad about it? 'Brit!' they yelled as I calmly jotted down the number 70004. 'Brit!' they shrieked, tossing each other's caps into the air and whooping like a troupe of Apache raindancers. I sat there, baffled and amused. Didn't I realize how lucky I was? they demanded. To see a Britannia on your first-ever trainspotting day. Complete jam! I was certainly 'a soddin' lucky bleeder!' agreed Bolt. But he was obviously pleased for me. He said that all the big passenger engines had a 4–6–2 wheel arrangement and smoke deflectors. I understood 4–6–2 easily enough, but I couldn't understand why that was called a 'pacific'. Bolt didn't know why – it just was, that's all. He was annoyed by my questions. It wasn't enough just to see a Britannia, I had to understand how important it was too.

They called it Steamer Gates, but by the time I arrived there I'd already missed the golden years of steam. It was a form of transport, and a way of life, already fingered for destruction on an immense scale. The Jubilees and Duck Sixes and Scots were on their way out, surrendering their territory to the diesels, the Bo-Bos and the Brush and the Peaks. With our bottles of pop, our notebooks and pens, even a secret cigarette or two, we were set up as witnesses to a swan song. We were children of the inter-regnum, caught in an uneasy period between the glories of the steam age and the cleaned-up corporate future.

Railwaymen were real men then, working-class heroes in faded indigo denim. They strolled past us, swinging their billycans full of tea (to be heated up later on their engine's firebox), smoking Woodbines, grumbling about their bosses. If they were in a good mood they greeted you with a nod and a wink. We loved being acknowledged. Every boy wanted to grow up and work alongside these men, as a driver preferably, or at least as a stoker or signalman.

There was a signal box at Steamer Gates. Signalling was another job that needed muscle. It was all done by wires in those days, long, long wires that ran through a complicated system of levers and pulleys to raise the red and yellow signals hundreds of yards away down the track. The man certainly had his work cut out, controlling a busy stretch of main line, and keeping an eye on a load of daft kids. A favourite trick, when he wasn't looking, was to jump down to the line nearest to us and put a penny on the rail. One of the long, slow coal trains that trundled past could turn a coin into a ready-polished medallion the size of a jam jar lid.

The main road sloped down under the railway and part of the signalman's job was to open the crossing gates for any vehicles that were too high to pass under the adjacent bridge. When there were no engines to look at, we often amused ourselves by throwing our jumpers into the photo-electric beam which set off the klaxons and the flashing message: DANGER – VEHICLE TOO HIGH. Cyclists and milk-float drivers knew damn well they were OK to get through, but they couldn't help stopping and scratching their heads and feeling guilty for setting off all the alarms.

*   *   *

Down the line from Steamer Gates was Anglesey Rec, a field of worn-out grass enclosed on three sides by railway lines. On the other side of the mesh fence the trains provided a constant background to the unruly football matches and messing about on swings. It was only natural for kids to take an interest. There was a car dump alongside the tracks too, and between trains we sat in the cars wrenching the steering wheels and growling like engines, jerking the long gearsticks, furiously winding the windows up and down (regardless of whether or not there was any glass left in). A long time before we had Mad Max there was Barmy Bolt, cruising the ruins of post-war England in his green Morris Minor.

In 1964 we were living in the last years of the iron age. Sometimes clanking past the Rec there'd be a sad procession: a Jubilee on its last-ever job, steaming its own way to the scrapyard, towing a couple of Duck Sixes, an Ozzie, a little Jinty. But we weren't really sad. They were numbers to be recorded and we were among the last boys to jot them down. We were privileged in an odd way. Anyway, these engines wouldn't really die. The molecules of iron and brass would be recycled. The chemistry teacher had said that matter could be neither created nor destroyed. There was karma. The old steamers would be buckled and crushed, sliced with oxy-acetylene. But pressed, stamped, melted and extruded, they'd live again, in teapots and fridge components and bicycle wheels, even in the staples that held our school exercise books together.

Across the line from Anglesey Rec, veiled by smoke, were 'the sheds'. Officially called Motive Power Depots, railway sheds were tantalizing but forbidden places. Burton had a huge MPD: two roundhouses side by side and a busy yard full of locos coaling-up or being cleaned. These were mostly commonplace 8-Freights and Blackies; but there was always the occasional 92-er, mightily impressive with its blinkered smokebox and its ten big driving wheels, and our small complement of Jubilees.

With Bolt as my guide, I quickly learned the art of 'bunking'. We had to walk the long ash-path from Steamer Gates, duck past the railwaymen's canteen, then dodge through a tiny door into one of the two round-houses. Such a small insignificant door, yet in that moment you slipped from a fresh-smelling open-air world into a strange sepulchral atmosphere, silent but for the hiss of escaping steam. This was the first time I'd been so close to a railway engine and, without a station plat-form to bring me level, I stood feeling small and awed by the scale of it. But how thoughtful of British Railways to arrange all these locos for the convenience of us spot-ters. One quick circuit of the turntable and you had another twenty numbers jotted down.

You weren't exactly welcome there, though. We slipped through another door into the second round-house, but Bolt decided it was too risky to go out into the depot yard; there were too many railwaymen around getting their engines ready for work. We went back the way we'd come, and as we passed the canteen a man in overalls shouted something along the lines of 'Bugger off you little buggers!'

On our next visit we even dared 'cab' some of the engines. Setting foot on board the ash-covered footplate entitled us to put a C for 'cabbed' next to that number in our *ABC Combined Volumes*. It didn't take me long to get addicted to the thrill of these guerilla raids into the heart of railway territory. Although we saw the shed foreman and the train crews as spoilsports, they must have had many a hairy moment with young kids dodging around between moving railway engines.

My friendship with Bolt was cut short in an unpleasant way. We'd been in a phone box for some reason – mere curiosity I expect – when the man from the Post Office came charging out and dragged us inside. He took our names and addresses and sent us away with a flea in our ear. That same evening the police visited both of us at home and told our parents that we'd been phoning 999. Each of us denied the charge, strenuously and tearfully, but no one believed us.

How could two harmless kids be treated so awfully? The only explanation I can think of is that Bolt was wearing a leather jacket with ROLLING STONES painted on the back. The Stones were bad news just then (hadn't they just pissed on a garage wall?) and any fans must have been hooligans by default. We were forbidden to go around together from then on. Protests were useless and, anyway, Bolt was destined for the sec mod, so I was unlikely to see him again. The summer holidays were over, and in those six weeks I'd had my basic grounding as a trainspotter. From then on I'd have to find my own feet.

It's always hard to say goodbye to your guru, so I didn't. I couldn't. Bolt had turned me on to trainspotting (and to the Rolling Stones) and it seemed like I owed him something, but I was too young to express those kinds of feelings. Anyway, how could I have guessed that a junior-school fad would change the whole course of my life?

Postscript. Twenty years later, browsing through the railway shelves in a second-hand book shop, I was astounded to find a photograph of Bolt and me. The book was a history of Derby Works and the photo depicted the 1964 Open Day and Flower Show. Our appearance was quite accidental, unwittingly snapped for posterity as we climbed up on the buffer beam of the day's star exhibit, Coronation 46245 *City of London*. It was a queer discovery and overwhelmed me with nostalgia. Normally, humanly, I might have bought the book, but some deep-seated superstition warned me off. I felt quite scared by these two ghosts from the sixties, that skinny eleven-year-old that was me and yet wasn't.

002   The Not So Great Great Western

As a Midlands kid, used to Duck Sixes and Blackies, my first sighting of a Great Western loco was a real thrill. Ironically, it wasn't at Bristol, Swindon or Paddington, or any of those famous Great Western places, indeed it wasn't on a trainspotting trip at all, but during a coach outing with my mum to Dudley Zoo.

Alongside the zoo was a disused station, still in use as a parcels depot, and when I saw a slow pillar of grey smoke breaking up over its wooden roof I made Mum take me down to have a look. And there was 7813 *Freshford Manor*, green and brassy through the latticed shadows, simmering quietly and in no great hurry. I tingled secretly. Not only had this loco got a quaint four-figure number (in 1948 every company except the GWR had been forced to add an extra digit to their loco numbers) but its name and numberplates were cast in gleaming brass. There was no one about, no activity on the platform, no sound except for the whisper of steam and, in the distance, the murmuring chorus of kids at the zoo. This enchanted moment is one that has remained with me in perfect detail for thirty years (so branded, in fact, that when I took my own children to Dudley Zoo a quarter of a century later, I could hardly bear the overwhelming feeling of nostalgia).

I underlined the number in my *ABC Combine* as soon as I got home, and for weeks it was my proudest exhibit. I'd sit staring at it for ages, but the more I looked, the more taunted I felt by its uniqueness; one thin red line in an otherwise unused section of the book. What about all these other GWR locos with such quintessential English names: *Witherslack Hall*, *Tudor Grange*, *Cadbury Castle*, *Hinton Manor*? To the bookish child that I was, it conjured up a weird and wonderful England populated by Agatha

25

Christie colonels, Wodehouse aunts and Elizabethan plotters. No doubt about it, I'd got a taste for the Great Western and I wanted to see more.

In 1965 Burton was still an important station, with a buffet and bookstall and a waiting room kept warm by a roaring coal fire. As well as the North–South expresses that passed through, we also had a local service to Wolverhampton, a direct line into GWR territory. One freezing January Saturday I set off aboard a rickety DMU, determined to add some Castles, Halls and Granges to my solitary Manor. DMU stood for diesel multiple unit, better known by kids as 'bog units'. A despised hybrid, these trains were neither carriage nor loco, and many spotters just couldn't be bothered with them. This was no-frills, bog-standard travel – hence the name. The smudgy windows rattled in their frames, any seat that wasn't weighted down by a bum vibrated, and engine fumes seemed to be purposely piped inside just to give you a chronic head. The one plus was that you could sit behind the driver and see the way ahead just as he did, watch his practised hand on the controls. As we slipped past the spires of Lichfield Cathedral and into the drab backdrop of the Black Country I felt as intrepid as all the explorers I'd read about in my books.

At Wolverhampton I hurried down from the High Level station to the Low Level; a real Great Western station, with chocolate and cream paintwork and the dusty smell of history. At the end of the platform was my next 4-figure cop: 7022 *Hereford Castle*, the first of two Castles seen that frosty day. It wasn't as pristine as *Freshford Manor* had been (these were working engines, after all) but even under the grime you could see it had pedigree. In the loco hierarchy a Castle had to be worth at least two Manors. I watched 7022 back on to a Paddington-bound express and yearned to be one of the lucky passengers.

Fortified by cups of BR tea and bridging the gaps with Cadbury's Snack (yes, I remember clearly; the finger ones, seven to a pack), I sat on a luggage trolley and thrilled to the steady parade of Granges and Halls which chugged in and out of the station. In between these smoke-shrouded entrances and exits, I watched a cheerful little pannier tank shunting parcels wagons.

My second Castle arrived early in the afternoon. But this one wasn't London-bound. Pulling half a dozen wagons with flapping tarpaulins, it limped through the station, leaking steam from its old machinery, shamefaced at its lowly duty. The grime was caked on so thickly you couldn't tell what colour it had been. This one, 5014, should have been *Goodrich Castle*, but where the name had been attached there were just three naked brackets, a sad sight with which I was to become familiar.

At teatime, I reluctantly headed back to the High Level to get the boring DMU back to boring old Burton. But I'd got the Great Western bug and I couldn't wait to spread the gospel.

The glory I missed. Spotters snap 6961 *Stedham Hall* in its prime at the head of a Paddington–Swansea express

If I hadn't palled up with him, Andy Parker might have been quite happy collecting stamps. Not serious stuff – just those gaudy stickers from Romania and Turkey – but he insisted it was a good hobby. He claimed he'd learned Russian from it. 'Noyta CCCP, da?'

I wasn't impressed. He might as well have recited Yuri Gagarin's name backwards.

Andy was aiming to join the school stamp club, but I knew he'd be unhappy in it. The stamp club was for bespectacled swots who specialized in Victorian definitives and South African triangulars. He'd be much happier coming trainspotting with me, I insisted. At least you didn't need your own tweezers to be taken seriously, and since his mum had just bought him a splendid duffel coat he might as well have an outdoor hobby to go with it. He thought it over for a while, but still needed convincing. I worked on him all the way home, and treated him to a fistful of Lemfizz cubes from the sweet shop. That clinched it. I had my first convert.

From Snow Hill, still a busy station in 1965, we caught one of the 'cat's whiskers' diesel trains to Tyseley. Breaking daylight and rattling past Moor Street station within sight of Birmingham's ugly tower blocks, we'd entered a looking-glass world where trains ran the wrong way, signals pointed downwards for go and the tracks were miles apart (a legacy of the GWR's ill-fated broad-gauge). Bordesley Green, Small Heath & Sparkbrook, the long, island stations passed by the window. Then there they were: Tyseley sheds. A rush to the window was followed by howls of protest because as soon as we sighted the rows of engines they were blocked out of view behind an embankment.

But never mind, the sheds were only a minute's walk from the station. It looked like an easy bunk too; there was no gaffer's office to dodge past, no drivers' canteen, just a wide gateway, through which we sauntered with ease. Crunching across the cinders, we lost ourselves in the sidings alongside the shed. Even if we never made it into the roundhouse itself, there were plenty of engines here, and with only 4-figure numbers to jot down we were looking at knocking a useful 20 per cent off the bunking time!

Missing nameplates I'd got used to, but so many of the numberplates had gone too, replaced by slapdash chalkings on the cabsides. I could tell Andy wasn't sold on the glories of the GWR and I had to admit it looked like a poor show. But then . . . here was a beauty, all shining green, red buffer-beam, polished numberplates. Prairie-tank 4555 wasn't a namer, true, but it gave me the chance to show Andy what I meant about the glorious GWR. Little did I know that this tarted-up loco was a privately owned showpiece destined for the museum. Anyway, the thrill of a successful bunk and a book full of cops soon made us forget our doubts.

Another bog unit took us back to Snow Hill and on past to Wolverhampton Low Level. According to the bunkers' bible, the *ABC Locoshed Directory*, Oxley sheds were a good hour's walk from the station. But another spotter put us right. The best way to get there, he told us, was on a local train to Dunstall Park, one stop down the line.

The station at which the two of us (and only the two of us) alighted was small and little used, hanging on bravely in the aftermath of Beeching. Over the wall were Wolverhampton's Stafford Road sheds, already closed and derelict by that time, and across the road were the old loco works, also abandoned. We scaled the rackety gates for a quick look around. Dim memories remind me that the place was littered with bits and bobs, worksplates certainly, numberplates perhaps, documents and dockets too – valuable records of the place in its hey-day. But there were no locos to see (and no emasculated King doing duty as a stationary boiler, as some wag had insisted) so we turned our noses up and went off to find Oxley sheds.

An odd thing about Oxley, one of the great 'cathedrals

of steam', is that you approached it from below. Walking alongside a mucky canal and through an arch, the engine sheds stood smouldering at the top of a steep cinder path. We were just setting off up the slope when a pair of crazed Alsatians ran at us, snapping viciously.

'Let's not bother with Oxley,' said Andy, skipping out of their range.

But they weren't British Railways guard dogs, they were from adjacent allotments, less concerned with trainspotters than guarding their master's prize Brussels.

Oxley had plenty of 9Fs and Blackies on shed, but we were more interested in its Granges and Halls, and it only took us a few minutes to amass a small collection. At the back of the sheds there was a scrap line, a sad collection of derelict carriages and rusting engines: tanks and 8Fs, a couple of Jubilees, even a Gresley V2 from the Eastern Region. Once rival engines from different regions, here they stood, rusting and ignored, coupled together in a last handshake.

Back at Dunstall Park, waiting for the train back to Wolverhampton, I recall the woody smell of the waiting room, the hiss of gas lamps. But its cuteness was its own death warrant; the station was as out of time as Adlestrop or Buggleskelly. A couple of teenagers came in and the girl bullied her younger brother into handing his Mintoes around. Andy and I were at an age where we fancied anyone in a skirt, but we soon forgot such thoughts when we heard our train coming and rushed out to see a dinky pannier tank pulling two coaches.

A great day all round, I thought, but not quite enough to convince Andy. The argument started over which one of us the girl with the Mintoes had fancied, but it quickly degenerated into a slanging match. He thought the Great Western was crap. But I wasn't surprised; I'd known all along that his loyalties lay elsewhere.

Inevitably, the rest of my Western trips were solo ones – to Tyseley and Oxley again, but also to Banbury and

Oxford. The underlinings in my *Combine* were beginning to join up. There were no longer isolated red lines here and there, but the unbroken rows which were the mark of a seasoned spotter. At Oxford, sitting with my back

Double chimney, double status. *Eastnor Castle* plods through Slough with a mixed freight

to the dreaming spires, I caught the very last Halls and Granges and had my first glimpse of Southern steam which came up from Poole and swapped engines at Oxford. The Snow Hill–Oxford line was still partially steam-operated, and on many of my trips I was lucky enough to have Granges and Halls for haulage. Would it always be like this, that the best trips were the ones where I had no witnesses?

A few months later the 'Great' adjective that had stuck to the Western Region for so many years was well and truly vanquished. The fires were dead, and at Oxford, Banbury and Tyseley the ashes were raked out for the last time. The pride had gone from the railwaymen's hearts years ago and now their fight to keep the GWR spirit alive was finally over. I'd had a tantalizing glimpse of the glories of the GWR, and I suppose I should have been grateful for that.

Five years later, well after the end of steam on British Railways, I went back to Snow Hill, derelict by then and full of echoes. I was supposed to be on a shopping trip with my girlfriend (the sister of a fellow train-spotter, of course) but I couldn't resist a last look at the old place.

'It stinks,' she said, stepping gingerly through the years of accumulated litter.

'I just want to look,' I said.

Judging by her scowls and curses, I was winding her up no end. But how could I explain my need to linger? I was fascinated by all the relics – the Waiting Room and Way Out signs, the stained timetables in the wrecked offices, the broken cups in the old buffet – and I could hardly bear to leave them behind. Souvenir collecting was an integral part of trainspotting. If only I'd had a van to cart it all away—

'Let's go,' she said, pacing the platforms, cursing her brother for getting her fixed up with a trainspotter. Jason King would never treat his secretary like this. He was a real man with manly pursuits, he didn't go round picking up soiled luggage labels and twittering about trains.

'Won't be long,' I assured her. At the age of sixteen I knew tons about railway timetables, but I had no idea about the timetables of romance, quite unaware of that crucial point when a woman's patience runs out.

'For flip's sake . . .'

But then she found a diversion. There was a dead pigeon on the platform, just feathers and a skeleton, really, which fascinated and repelled her. It would have looked great on the cover of an Agatha Christie book, but I could only watch with horror as she brought down the heel of her boot and crushed the poor thing's eggshell skull. It was an omen. She was the first girlfriend who'd allowed any heavy petting, but I knew I could never be happy with someone who got so bored in derelict railway buildings.

003   Crewe: The Trainspotter's Mecca

I'd had my first glimpse of it in late 1964, passing through on a day trip to Rhyl with my mum. I'd half-expected it, but it took my breath away. Ambling in from the Derby line, the tracks suddenly came at us from all sides, switching, meshing, taking the simple perspective of one railway track and weaving a tangled magic carpet. Here was absolute railwayness on all sides; rails below us, electric wires above. A sprawling soot-clouded depot slipped away to the left before I even had chance to gasp. It was as overwhelming as a holy vision.

But the train wasn't stopping. If the vision made me laugh with joy, it quickly turned into a kind of hysteria. Dashing from window to window, crunching everyone's toes, I couldn't take it all in at once: black steamers with the brassy glint of nameplates, green big-nosed diesels, blue electrics kissing the overhead wires with a crack of sparks. The numbers danced in front of me and quickly slipped away. My hand was epileptic, juddering with ecstasy. I'd seen ten, twenty, thirty locos in as many seconds, and as we curved away on the line to North Wales I looked at my notebook. All I'd managed to record, in the large wild scribbles of a child, was a mere half a dozen numbers.

Back at school I told Andy Parker all about it, burbling with evangelical fervour. I had to go to Crewe again and he had to come with me. I had to have a witness. But his parents wouldn't let him go. He must have kept working on them though, for not long afterwards his dad volunteered to take us in the family car, a fat black Wolsley. I wasn't so keen on being chaperoned, but at least, as Andy pointed out, it would be free.

And so one Saturday we drove off for the sixty-mile trip. It all seemed a bit formal – approaching by car, buying a platform ticket, Andy's dad deciding which platform would give us the best vantage point. But down on the station it was just like I'd remembered it. Mr Parker intended to keep us on a firm rein though; we could join the dozens of well-behaved spotters standing at the end of the platform, but there was no way he was going to sanction any shed-bunking. If he'd been my dad I would probably have screamed at him, but I could only suffer in polite silence. (Looking back, I know it would have been unthinkable for any responsible dad to encourage trespassing.) So near and yet so far . . . Across from the station we could see dozens of Britannias, Jubilees and Scots simmering in the yard of Crewe North shed. If only we'd had a pair of binoculars. One or two of the older spotters did have and generously passed their info on to less fortunate kids.

This first trip didn't yield much in the way of boastable trophies. There were plenty of Blackies and Jinties knocking about the station, but we had enough of those back home. Namers were what we all came to Crewe for. It wasn't just the number of locos that mattered, but the royalty of them. I knew quite well now how lucky I'd been to see Britannia 70004 on that first day, and I wanted more. Confined to the platforms, we only got to see two Britannias (70048 and 70051), taking my total to three. But we did get to see one of the last Royal Scots (46128 *The Lovat Scouts*), and stood alongside as it took over a Carlisle express from the roaring diesel that had brought it up from Euston.

I had to go again. Four weeks later I did. And on my own – as I had to be if I was going to bunk the sheds and get any decent cops. Free from the shackles of adult supervision, I bunked Crewe North (though I didn't

Andy Parker poses alongside a Deltic nameplate at
Grantham, 1965

realize at the time how lucky I'd been), Crewe South
and the diesel depot. In half an hour I copped not a
couple of Britannias, but a dozen or more – a quarter of
the class. For the first time I saw a chance of getting the
whole set; there were only fifty-five Britannias, and since
they were only fifteen years old British Railways
wouldn't be scrapping them for a while yet . . .

Before long, Crewe was attracting a regular gang of
us from grammar school. In parties of two, three, four
we joined the dozens – hundreds – of spotters who
roamed the platforms every Saturday. Derby to Crewe
was a slow journey, stopping at every titchy station, but
we had the sheds at Stoke to look out for. (I remember
one Saturday in particular, the day after the Aberfan
disaster. Darb sat with his feet up reading the Daily
Mirror and tutting. 'Poor little bastards,' he said. Trite
if well-meant sentiments, but I couldn't understand why
the children who had just died should be described as
bastards.)

If there was a trainspotting 'A-team' it was Andy,

Darb, Pipsqueak and me. There was an occasional half-hearted 'guest' – outsiders like Fat Harry, dandruffed and bad-tempered, so desperate for company they'd suffer any boredom. But their ignorance of railways and, worse, their unwillingness to learn, only made us despise them more. As for the A-team, we all came from quite different homes: Andy Parker's dad had the Wolsley and a stereogram in a polished walnut cabinet; Pipsqueak lived in a terraced house jam-packed with brothers and the smell of cooking; Darb's dad was in charge of the local playing fields and they lived in a flat over the adjacent café; and I lived in a council flat with my mum. Despite these differences, we were a cheerful bunch, and if there were any yawning gulfs between the wealth and status of our families then we never talked about them.

Yet a class divide did exist. It was remarkable that none of the kids from the school's A-stream were into trainspotting; it still seemed to have a class label stuck to it and wasn't deemed a suitable hobby for the sons of doctors, solicitors and shop-owners. Nor for earnest pupils like Melvin Bugg, whose mother had written to warn the headmaster that Melvin was 'hypersensitive', and should be treated kindly. I liked Bugg, but I knew that Crewe was no place for mummy's boys.

Looking at train magazines now, especially the steam nostalgia ones, I can't help but notice how many of the writers and photographers are doctors, clergymen and professors. It would be interesting to know if they are working-class kids who crossed the class system, or A-streamers who repressed their trainspotting instincts to please their parents and had to wait until adulthood to give full rein to their enthusiasm. If the latter is the case, do they feel any twinges of guilt? Probably not. Steam train enthusiasm, devoid now of its old repu-

Star turn. 46128 *The Lovat Scouts* heads out of Crewe
with an express for Carlisle

tations, is a genteel, slightly eccentric pursuit, one that's quite in keeping with the culture of the English middle classes.

The most amazing thing about Crewe is that it really didn't exist before the railways. A halt was built there to serve the stately home of Lord Crewe and it seemed like it might also make a good place for a junction for lines to Liverpool and Manchester, North Wales and the Midlands. The place grew by a kind of industrial symbiosis. It was almost a natural organism: one shed, two sheds, a loco works, a diesel depot, an electric depot.

Without adult supervision, we had no qualms about bunking the sheds. Crewe North (5A) was virtually impregnable. Arguably the most important depot in the country, there was no way any self-respecting shedmaster would put up with a bunch of scruffs running around amongst his fleet of Britannias, Jubilees and Coronations. Which, of course, was exactly what attracted the kids in the first place. But it was a safety thing too: Crewe North was on the go all the time, with engines forever moving in and out of the sheds, coaling-up, arriving from the station. For railwaymen it was a hazardous place, for careless kids it could be lethal. At 5A it wasn't just a matter of being thrown out by the gaffer; the depot was so important that patrolling it was down to the railway police. Once, one caught Andy and me on the footbridge that led to the sheds. We denied any intention of bunking, but the policeman sneered in disbelief.

'Don't think you can pull the wool over my eyes.'

We smirked and Andy piped up, 'Why? Are they issuing you with wool-lined helmets now?'

He got a clip round the ear for his cheek. But it was an acceptable hazard of trainspotting and we'd never have dreamt of getting nasty. You got caught, you got your ear clipped, and that was the way things were.

All the more surprising then that I managed to bunk Crewe North unheeded on that first solo visit. Bunking stories are still a regular theme in the letters pages of

Steam Railway and *Steam World*, and most of the writers say how they got kicked out of Crewe North. I put down my success to mere luck, but it's a badge I still wear with pride. Naturally, it had to be the one time I went to Crewe on my own, so no one ever believed me. The thing is, after all these years and so much scepticism, you find yourself wondering if you really did do it after all, or whether it's just a displaced memory, a fantasy adventure cobbled together from half-remembered snippets and photographs in magazines . . .

Crewe South and the nearby diesel depot were much easier as security was quite lax. If Crewe North was big, Crewe South was even bigger; a great sprawling yard of engines. The yard had no obvious design, hence surveillance was virtually impossible, and the dozen lines of engines were so long it made the place into a smoky maze where you rarely encountered anyone in authority.

Sitting on Crewe station could never get boring. There was, quite literally, never a dull moment. But it had one slight drawback; there was no single spot at Crewe where you could stand and catch all the action. If you were at the Northern end you missed all the locals at the Derby and Shrewsbury end; if you were on the Eastern side you missed trains on the far side; and all the freight trains were routed along a separate line that sped through a deep cutting at the side of the station (the only way you could get those numbers was to sneak on to the Crewe North footbridge and peer down). The only sure way to keep tabs was to be in constant patrol, walking from one end of the station to the other, an exhausting routine when you'd done it fifty times in one day.

Sometimes we took our own sandwiches, but we often visited the buffet for a packet of crisps or a Cornish pasty. There were the machines too, of course. It's a truism that all drinks from machines are foul, but I rather liked the chicken soup. It looked like steaming urine with green tinsel floating in it – and my friends groaned whenever they glimpsed a cup – but I'd been weaned on Oxo drinks made with the mineral-rich water from cooked cabbage, so I loved it.

At the end of every big trip we went home, tired and happy, with our books full of scribbled numbers, pages curled at the corners, stained with oil and smoky fingerprints. In many ways, the best bit was yet to come: the creation of order out of chaos. Our disorderly lists of cops had to be processed, each one slotted into its appropriate place in the *ABC Combine* and marked with its red underline. In this way, each number became a memory, encrypted, filed away in numerical order. I tried to do mine as soon as I got home, if I felt up to it, or else I'd leave it until Sunday morning and lie full spread on the carpet while I listened to *The Clitheroe Kid* and waited for Sunday dinner.

I prided myself on my neatness. While other kids messed their books up with the first biro that came to hand – blue, green, red, even pencil – I stuck firmly to red. What's more, I took as much care as possible to make sure each underline was exactly the same length.

But it wasn't always a matter of marking one number off in one book. Besides the *Combine*, some kids still insisted on having separate copies of the steam, diesel and electric books that made up the *Combine*, all of which had to be kept up to date. Then there was the *Locoshed Book*, a vital accessory that listed every single engine yet again, this time with details of its home depot. And if you'd bunked a new shed on your travels, that had to be underlined too – once in the *Combine*, again in the *Locoshed Book* and yet again in the *Locoshed Directory* (which I'll come to later).

As well as all this, for a couple of years in 1965 and 1966, I also copied the contents of my scruffy notebooks into two big desk diaries which I'd ruled off especially for the purpose. It was as time-consuming as illustrating medieval manuscripts, but once done, with more neatness than I'd ever spare for my schoolwork, the satisfaction was priceless.

I knew of spotters who recorded things in even further depth, noting all kinds of details: how fast a train was going, how many carriages or wagons it had on, whether it was late, and even, if they knew the local train crews, who was driving it. It's tempting to regard this obsession with detail as futile and sad, but I knew some of these kids myself and they had otherwise healthy interests in girls, football, pop and fashion – so this amassing of details about the railways was just part of the general fun of being young. And yes, I did say fun.

Crewe doesn't have much magic now. It's as if that mysterious sprawling bazaar has been turned into a neat and well-behaved shopping mall. It can't be called a Mecca any more; it's more like a small chapel at the wayside, a place to worship with quiet desperation. Crewe is still an important place on the railway map, but not half as much as it used to be, to travellers or to trainspotters. There's no longer the need for all the changeovers that made it such a bustling place – diesels handing over to steam, steam to electric, electric to diesel – with a constant stream of passengers scurrying from one platform to another to make their connections. A child might still be awed by its size, but they wouldn't get dizzy on its glorious cocktail of fumes. Maybe that's all it was in the end, just some kind of chemical addiction. We thought we'd gone to pay our childish tribute to history, but really we were just the unwitting heralds of solvent abuse.

Trainspotting doesn't normally offer much opportunity: for star-spotting. But I did once speak to P. B. Whitehouse at Crewe.

Trainspotting does, however, have an establishment: a score or so of men who've been around since before nationalization and are still held in awe by their juniors. I think it's partly to do with the double-barrelled names and anonymous initials (Pat Ransome-Wallis, G. Freeman Allen, Cecil J. Allen, L. T. C. Rolt, C. Hamilton

Ellis, W. J. V. Anderson) and partly because of their bespectacled and avuncular appearance, and the fact they seemed to know everything. But there's never been any snobbery. Trainspotting has always been a democracy, embracing all men, from right scruffs to Right Honourables. No names, no pack-drill. Unlike the golf club or the Chamber of Trade, no one cares about your income, your profession, or who you know. What you know about trains is what counts. It's one of the few areas where you'll see professors comparing notes with latch-key kids.

(It's worth remarking that, up until the sixties, a lot of trainspotters wore ties and even the scruffs kept up this semi-groomed image with their sec-mod neckwear. It sounds silly and impossibly cute – but not if you remember that even The Rolling Stones wore ties when they first started out.)

The one we all wanted to meet was the late Eric Treacy, Bishop of Wakefield. We knew that, for some reason, railways attracted the clergy, but a bishop was something special. Would he be wearing his mitre and carrying his crook, or would he be in plain-clothes, the only clue being a slightly too purple shirt?

Many of the old guard have passed on now and the genteel establishment has dwindled. But of the few that remain they all seem to be comfortably well off and own engines all over the place. The nearest trainspotting now has to a benevolent uncle is Pete Waterman, the millionaire record producer, a man who's so loaded that he seems to be buying a loco or a set of carriages every other week.

004   Sir Nigel Gresley's Spearmint Seagull

Since I'd dragged Andy across the Black Country on a Great Western wild-goose chase, it seemed only fair I should return the favour by joining him on a trip to the

East Coast main line at Grantham (a town famous with trainspotters a long time before it produced its blue-rinse prime minister).

Though consciously having little choice in the matter, Andy was a fierce champion of the old LNER. His grandad had filled him with tales of a boyhood by the wonderful King's Cross–Edinburgh line: eye-witness accounts of *Mallard* on its record-breaking run, V2s on express freights, the Flying Scotsman whistling its way towards the Borders. I loved the GWR, but the LNER was even more important to Andy; he'd been fed the propaganda with his cornflakes. Loyalty to the LNER was a filial duty: at least one of the children had to be groomed in it, one of them had to carry the myths and legends into the seventies and beyond. Even if the next generation ended up living in a pressurized bubble on

One of the last of the legendary Streaks: 60019 *Bittern* on a spotters' special at Derby in 1965

the moon, the LNER would not be forgotten. After all, the children would still need some bedtime stories.

So off we set one Saturday, just the two of us, with Andy taking over the role as guide. From Nottingham we took a jerky DMU from the old Victoria station, a cavernous place with a high glass roof stained by the black breath of decades. It had been an important stop on the Great Central, but the expresses had all been replaced by sporadic 'semi-fasts' (a clumsy euphemism for semi-slow and annoying). The long platforms were empty now and the whole place had the dank smell of doom hanging over it. I was spookified and couldn't wait to depart. Beetling our way into the mouth of the tunnel, we crossed one of those invisible thresholds in the space-time-railways continuum, slipping away from the familiar sights of the Midlands into something Eastern and vaguely mysterious.

There were no steamers left at Grantham, the Streaks and Peppercorn A1s were long gone. BR's Eastern Region had welcomed the diesel age wholeheartedly and the only steam to come out of King's Cross now was that which escaped from the tea urn in the buffet. A handful of those legendary express engines survived, but they'd been banished to Aberdeen to be used on fish trains and local passenger's, too far away for us to go and see. Even if we could have afforded it, would Andy have wanted the humiliation? *Mallard*, had it still been in service, would have been lucky to get a job taking half a dozen milk tankers from Arbroath to Dundee. I didn't lose my chance to irritate Andy with childish taunts about the old supremos of the LNER, Sir Nigel Grizzly and A. H. Pepperpot. Wouldn't they have simply died to see their wonderful locos taking old ladies into Dundee to do their shopping?

Still, if the golden days of the LNER were gone, I had to admit that the Deltics were one hell of a sight. You should have seen them; roaring through the narrow confines of Grantham station they rattled the tea-cups in the buffet and pushed along a tumbleweed of wind that fluttered all the newspapers on the bookstall. Thunder and chaos and speed, just the kind of thrill no schoolboy could resist, even the ones who claimed to be unreconstructed steam fans. Nothing ever went very fast through Burton (Steamer Gates overlooked a railway equivalent of a road-hump which would have sent any speeding trains into orbit), but at Grantham they came through like beasts from hell, 106 tons of green and yellow. 'Passengers are advised to stand well back from the edge of the platform,' warned the loudspeakers, and if they knew what was good for them they did just that. The slipstream of a passing express was quite capable of whipping off a hat or two and would have tossed a doddering pensioner or unwary child about like a rag doll. Respect was the key-word and we made sure we were always on our best behaviour.

Andy would have liked me to see *Golden Plover* at the head of The Flying Scotsman, just for the satisfaction of seeing my jaw drop in admiration. But I'd have had my teeth wired rather than give him the satisfaction. Secretly though, I had to admit that these Deltics were something else. But there was no way I was going to let on. Not after he'd been so humphy about the Great Western.

So who was a diesel-lover now? It hadn't even crossed my mind, but that was the accusation levelled at me by some of the die-hards back in class 2C at the Grammar. Pipsqueak, who came from a family of steam fans, was most disappointed in me. Granted, it was hard to avoid diesels altogether by then, but why go somewhere where there was nothing else but? He'd refused point-blank to visit Grantham with us, it would have been anathema and a waste of precious pocket money. I understood his reasoning and I admired his loyalty – but I elected to take a more pragmatic attitude. It would have been churlish in the extreme to cock a snook at such spectacular sights as the Deltics just because of some hazy ethical stance.

Like it or not, Andy and I were now children of the diesel age. Neither of us had ever known the real GWR or LNER, so it was left to us to pick up the cudgels on behalf of our respective regions. We couldn't race Castles against A4s, so it had to be Westerns against Deltics, and I hated to admit it, but the Deltics won hands down as far as power and thrills were concerned. (Still, to be fair, I'd not yet seen the Western Region's diesel-hydraulics at speed.)

But Grantham wasn't just Deltics. Halfway through the quiet afternoons there was always a Pullman train, an elongated flash of brown and cream coaches and a flickering glimpse of brass light fittings, white tablecloths and silver teaspoons. It was as if a train from another age had slipped through a loophole in the space-time fabric. The Pullman carriages all had fancy names – *Amethyst* and *Topaz*, *Medusa* and *Pegasus* – and it was permissible for trainspotters to collect them because they were special. An impossible task! Writing down unfamiliar names which were flashing past at 80 m.p.h. was as daft as collecting leaves in a wind tunnel. We tried to be methodical, each of us jotting down each alternate carriage, but we always got mixed up somehow. ('I thought I was getting the odd ones and you were getting the evens!')

Occasionally one of the Deltics deigned to stop at Grantham and we sprinted to the end of the platform for a closer look. The yukkiest thing was the yellow warning panels on the front end, black and sticky with splattered flies and assorted gnats. These mighty engines were like giant swatters sweeping through the Lincolnshire countryside. Standing alongside one, we felt almost as small and vulnerable as the flies. Even at rest the Deltics commanded respect. And when they revved up for the off, we hooted with delight. The platform trembled and we could feel the vibrations through our lace-up shoes, groping up our legs, filling our guts with queasiness.

There was another curious working most afternoons: two of the Southern Region's Crompton diesels, which had come all the way from the London suburbs at the head of a Blue Circle cement train. These kinds of quirky timetabling were always a delight, giving us a chance

106 tons of throbbing power: a Deltic waits for the off at Grantham, 1965

to cop engines from the other end of the country without having to make any effort. And it was all the better if it worked in your favour; spotters in Woking or Southampton would have to wait until hell froze over before they ever got a visit from a Deltic or a Peak.

What Grantham didn't have, though, was any railway sheds to bunk. We couldn't go trespassing, slipping through gaps in fences or clambering over gates. There was no adventure. At Wolverhampton we'd been interlopers. At Grantham we were polite spectators; still reverent, but distant and uninvolved. If we'd had any money we could have hopped on one of the trains and taken a quick spin behind one of those Deltics to Peterborough or Doncaster.

One thing I did like about the old LNER (again, I never admitted as much to Andy) was the refreshing absence of toadying. On the Great Western and the London Midland all the engines had been named after castles and kings, colonies and regiments, stately homes and safe old poets like Tennyson and Hardy. Railways were, at the end of the day, part of the establishment. And so trainspotting got tied up with patriotism and

British values in a big way. But the LNER – and I only had the old spotting books to go by – had had a wild imagination. Their engines were named after birds (*Wild Swan*, *Kingfisher*, *Mallard*), Walter Scott characters (*Madge Wildfire*, *Guy Mannering*), or even, gloriously louche, famous racehorses with names like *Captain Cuttle*, *Spearmint* and *Blink Bonny*. I imagined two LNER directors sitting in the bar at Kempton Park, sticking a pin in *Sporting Life* then ringing up the Doncaster Works foreman to get the nameplates made.

Trainspotting aside, I really enjoyed getting around. I'd travelled the Silk Route with Marco Polo and sailed round the Horn with Magellan, yet I scarcely knew my own country. Slowly I built up a jigsaw: the ramshackle workshops of the Black Country, the pottery kilns of Stoke, the creepy fields of Lincolnshire. But was it a happy land? With each trip we were faced, more and more, with the railways' twilight, the evidence plentiful and irrefutable. Lines were being closed, steam engines were filthy and neglected. Yet we clung to the myths and legends, defending our adopted companies with fierce but gentlemanly loyalty. And old spotters still argue the odds over halves of bitter and clacking dominoes in the clubs: whether Gresley was a better railway chief than Stanier, whether the A4s were smoother runners than the Coronations, whether LNER drivers were friendlier to young spotters than those of the LMS.

005 My Brilliant Backyard: Burton, 1966

The grammar school had clubs for stamp collectors, chess buffs and radio hams, and even a French Society for bilingual swots – but there was nothing on offer for trainspotters. We knew we were beyond the pale; it wasn't the kind of activity a grammar school wanted to encourage. But even if such a club had existed I doubt if anyone would have joined it. The last thing we wanted was to be officially approved, to have club outings on which we were supervised by an off-duty geography teacher with a Flying Scotsman biro.

They say the old grammar schools were built on hills as a kind of symbolic challenge – that you'd have to work hard to get to the top. It may be true, but the best thing about the lofty position of our school was that, in the right classroom, you had a view over the whole town and could see the main line like a silver wire glinting in the sun. It may have been too far away to see any numbers, but you could tell the greenness of a diesel or the blackness of a steamer. When lessons got too boring I stared dreamily out of the window and doodled on my exercise books. Maths teachers aren't known for their kindliness and they went mad when I handed books in. Not only was the homework half-baked, the doodles were totally irrelevant. If I'd drawn protractors and stylized formulae I might have got away with it, but a Britannia with three dinky coaches was just too much.

Though we often moaned about the predictability of Burton's rail traffic, in reality we were quite lucky. In other towns the kids just stood by the line and watched the trains go past, left to right or right to left. Boring. But Burton's brewing industry had spawned a maze of lines and shunting yards in the town. Steamer Gates was still our main meeting place, but there were plenty of other good locations.

Little Burton Bridges

Andy and I walked to school and back every day. A good two miles, but we thought nothing of it. Mornings were always a rush, since we were always late, but the evenings were a glorious dawdle. Every day was a laugh of some sort and there were plenty of corner shops to call in at for sweets, pop or ciggies. Most days we'd stop off at Little Burton Bridges for a while. Little Burton was a dark and faintly dangerous place, a community of about a dozen tiny houses jam-packed together alongside the railway arches, with some of the bedrooms literally inches from the shunting yards. How the hell did anyone sleep in these slums? Yet we couldn't help feeling a bit of envy for the kids who lived there, so close to the action.

There'd always be at least one train passing through, always chance of a cop. As often as not, though, it'd just be an Ozzie on a coal train. Built by the War Department to an Austerity design (hence the name), Ozzies were big and drab and clumsy, unloved by spotters and railwaymen alike. We took the numbers down, but we felt no affection for them. (How guilty I feel now about hating them so much – I'd love to see one again. I'd be so respectful.)

One teatime we were kicking our heels waiting for something interesting to happen (rather, Andy was kicking his heels, I was kicking idly at the derelict fence, rubbing splinters of wood off with the sole of my shoe), when an old gent stopped to watch us.

'Any expresses?' he asked.

We shook our heads. He came nearer and we could smell his breath, a sickly blast of old bread and chocolate.

'Any railway hooligan specials?' he demanded nastily. 'Any cattle trucks for teenage shit?' He began to swing his shopping bag round like a propeller, bringing it in sharp contact with my head. 'That's for defiling British Railways property,' he snarled, making a grab for my sweaty collar as we fled.

Within the general Steamer Gates crowd there were always rivalries and shifting alliances, short-lived feuds and recognized pecking-orders. The regional loyalties were fairly permanent (that was hardest to change, once chosen) but it was not unknown for someone whose favourite engines were Britannias to turn up next day and claim Jubilees had always been their Number One. Such foibles were tolerated, mildly mocked, but soon forgotten. The biggest cause of friction though was the old steam versus diesel debate.

Diesels could never be as alive as steamers, they didn't work by the same dirty and elemental chemistry. All the same, I couldn't hate them as assiduously as Pipsqueak did. For one thing, Britain's railway workshops (still a dozen of them even then) were busy building the future and we trainspotters had the privilege of seeing many of these diesels spanking new, fresh out of Derby or Crewe. That feeling of being one of the first kids ever to see a loco was quite special. More importantly, if trainspotting was about collecting numbers, we knew that it should be possible to get a full set of Peaks or Bo-Bos or Baby Brush. Unlike those lucky Northern kids of the late fifties/early sixties, we'd never get all our Jubilees or Scots or Coronations – we'd started too late and lived in the wrong area. (Even when I did get close to finishing a steam class – I needed only six of the Britannias – British Rail went and scrapped the very ones I wanted. I was heartbroken and dead mad.) At least with diesel we stood a chance.

But if Andy and I disagreed with Pipsqueak about the pros and cons of dieselization, at least we were united about one thing – we hated those kids who actually loved diesel in preference to everything else. There was something about these diesel-lovers that bugged all of us. It was their superior kind of smiles, their positive glee about the approaching end of steam, their constant harping on about the engineering merits of diesel.

They were lepers. But worse, they were lepers with the gift of clairvoyance. We knew darned well they were right. But even so, even if steam engines were on their last legs they deserved our loyalty. We couldn't just cast them aside for the sleek green seductive charms of diesel. We gave these traitors names and put them on a black-list: the Scottish Brush Kid, the Bo-Bo Bleeder, and the Shunter Bloke; all outcasts whose company we shunned with conscientious resolve. Yet it didn't matter to them that they were hated: these were the kind of people who were always desperate to be on the winning side, the swots who always had to get full marks. Being right was far more important than loyalty to a peer group and an outdated mode of transport.

Fudgers were equally despised. These kids were so desperate for attention, they filled their books with fraudulent underlinings. They claimed, at the age of twelve or thirteen, that they went on unaccompanied trips to the North of Scotland to see engines that we could only dream of (*Kingfisher* or *Sun Chariot*). They told us they had an understanding with the shedmaster at Aberdeen; he used to drink with their dad, so the son was always welcome to call in whenever he felt like it. Sometimes we half believed these tales – there were parents who let their children roam the country like gypsies – but when the same kids said they had to be in for six or they'd get told off we just fell about laughing.

Every class of steam loco had an official or unofficial name. Those not grand enough to be officially recognized as a Hall, a Jubilee or a Britannia would be christened by the drivers or the kids at the lineside. And so we had 8-Freights, Ozzies, Blackies, Duck Sixes and Crabs among others. Many of the nicknames varied from region to region; Blackies in Burton were Mickeys to the kids on Merseyside. The diesels also had names; approved ones such as Peaks, Warships, Deltics and Westerns, and nicknames such as Tats, Bo-Bos, Baby Deltics, Whistlers, Hoovers and Growlers, most of which were derogatory reflections on performance. Nicknaming is an assertion not only of the trainspotter's right to be judgemental, but also of his need to feel involved in the culture.

We were not oblivious to the times we were living in. This was 1966. Music was part of our lives. Bolt had turned me on to the Stones and I'd become a bigger fan than he was. In the evenings someone would bring along a portable radio, and between trains we'd sit listening to Radio Luxembourg. One evening Jimmy Savile played the whole of the Stones' new LP *Aftermath*, and the steamers clanked by with their coal trains to a soundtrack of 'Baby, baby, baby, you're out of time . . .'

Wetmore Sidings

Even trainspotters need a secret place. I still visited Steamer Gates and the Iron Bridges, but Wetmore Sidings was nearer home, and I spent most of my evenings there. There were sidings on both sides of the track, so when there was nothing on the main line I could sit and watch the Jinties shunting beer wagons. Shunting must have been repetitive and boring for the men whose job it was, but for me it was repetitive and fascinating. No matter how many times the Jinty or the fat diesel-shunter went through the same procedure, it was always fun to watch the loose wagon gliding driverless and brakeless along the line. But these men knew what they were doing; each wagon connected just hard enough to set up a relay of clanging buffers along the rest of the train.

The old steamers were truly living things, with foibles and character, but their health was a cause of increasing concern. Sometimes they put on an impressive show of bravado, barking like beasts from the gates of hell, but it was a fierceness born of pain. Close up you could hear the loose bits clanking and see the steam leaking from places it shouldn't have. But some were still cared for by their drivers and firemen. Cleaned up and lovingly oiled, they could purr so softly you were unaware of them until they were underneath your feet, blasting smoke and soot up through the loose planks of the footbridge. I loved that, it was like an instant Turkish bath.

Few other trainspotters troubled me at Wetmore. There'd been some there in the past, though. The planks on the bridge were etched with engine numbers and names with a slightly threatening ring: Gaz, Kev, Duggy. But whoever they were, they didn't go there any more. I was king of the castle now. As well as standing guard on the footbridge, I'd built myself a simple eyrie by wedging an old sleeper across the joists which supported the wooden stairway.

Usually it was just me, but I did have an occasional visitor. One was a slightly subnormal bloke by the name of Trevor. He turned up one day with a packet of Refreshers and handed me one as we watched the Jinty shunting wagons.

'You don't have to crunch 'em,' he said. 'I know a bloody good-value trick. Get a cup off your mum, mash up half a dozen Refreshers with the handle of a knife, then fill it up with water.' He looked at me, as if expecting applause. 'A whole drink of pop from a threepenny packet of tuffies!'

He was harmless enough, but I was glad he wasn't a regular visitor. I was jealous of my territory and I always bristled whenever anyone appeared at the far end of the bridge. It was a public right of way, after all, but with the narrowness and enforced closeness I had a Little John complex about having to defend myself against interlopers.

I was allowed to stay out until about 8.20, the time of the mail train for Bristol. When that rushed through in a blur of red and clattered into the distance, I'd head off home to watch *The Avengers* or *The Saint*. Burton's rail traffic was fairly predictable – mainly 8Fs, Blackies, Ozzies, 92-ers – but there were surprises. One evening, when the mail train had passed and I was about to head off, the clang of signals going up tempted me to stay on. It was getting dark by then, but I didn't have to wait long. I could see the smoke, and whatever it was was approaching pretty damn fast. The plume of white and grey swirled nearer, got squashed with a roar of protest under the road bridge, and a thrill shot through me as a Scot hurtled through on a fast goods. The only trouble was it was too dark to see what its number was. Not surprisingly, when I told them at school the next day they refused to believe me. The dreaded word fudger was whispered. I even started to doubt myself. Had I seen it, or had it been just a mirage, a trick in the twilight?

Stretton Junction

We could see some trains from the front window of our first-floor council flat. It wasn't the main line, just a freight branch that went the long way round to Derby. It wasn't very busy either, but there were always a few trains in the early evenings, not long after I'd got home from school.

You knew when one was coming, long before it actually appeared. The line was on a curved gradient out of Wetmore Sidings, so the engines struggled, sending clouds of smoke up over the rooftops. Many a time, having just sat down for tea, I'd fling down my knife and fork and dash out in the hope of catching a B1 clanking its way along to Eggington Junction.

The B1s were fairly ordinary freight engines, but the fact that they came from the Eastern Region made them worthy of attention. The kids in Nottingham and Doncaster probably despised them, but we welcomed the two or three that strayed our way each month. A lot of them were named after antelopes: *Springbok*, *Chamois*, *Wildebeest* and *Klipspringer*. A great idea. Spoilt, though, when they ran out of antelopes. They should have stopped there, but instead they used the drab monikers of railwaymen: *Geoffrey Gibbs*, *Leslie Runciman* and the suspiciously improbable *A. Harold Bibby*. And who was Fitzherbert Wright? He sounded like one of the toffs out of *The Magnet*. I was hoping to catch *Gnu* one of those days. It must have been the shortest nameplate on any locomotive – they'd had to put extra spaces between the letters just to make the whole thing long enough to put two bolts in.

Panicked by the idea of missing a cop, the race was on. 'Get stuffed!' I yelled at the kiddies who wanted me to stop and play tick with them. Then it was a hop, skip and a jump across the allotments to the abandoned trackbed which ran behind our house. From there I had a clear run up to meet the freight branch at Stretton Junction.

A clear run? Abandoned railways are not the best running tracks. There are dents every yard where the sleepers once lay, odd bits of cast-iron to stub your feet on and brambles running everywhere to send you sprawling headlong in the gravel and clinker.

It never was *Gnu* of course. I'd sit there, panting and croaking, proud to have won the race, only to find it was some crummy 8-Freight I'd already got. I hadn't even got the breath to shout 'Scrap it!' I could see the signalman laughing at me up in his box. There's something to be done about that lad, he'd think, reaching for his tea and reflecting on the madness of trainspotters in general.

Drained of adrenalin, I felt nervous now. A tramp nicknamed Barabas was rumoured to live in an abandoned air-raid shelter just down from the junction. What if my running past had disturbed his kip? I was terrified he would appear like a greasy string-tied shadow of death, blocking the path between me and the safety of home.

Exhausted as I was, I scrambled down the embankment and took the long way back. In reality, it was my mum I should have been scared of. Back home she would be scraping the plate of cold spaghetti and sauce-sodden toast into the bin and threatening that I'd never be given a meal again.

A telescope would have saved me an awful lot of trouble.

The Iron Bridges

I never did understand why it was called the Iron Bridges, since there was only one bridge. Pedantry aside, the lattice bridge commanded a good view of Burton's railway action, all the way to the station one way, to Wetmore Sidings in the other direction.

There was very little violence on the trainspotting scene. If you were a spotter you were more or less OK, at least with anyone else who shared your love of trains. You were safe enough at Steamer Gates, but away from there, at places like Iron Bridges, you could be picked on by lads with other interests. Football fans, for instance. Being a grammar-school boy was bad enough (enough to get you a smack in the gob any day), but to

Feel that steam up your trousers. An 8-Freight passes beneath the Iron Bridges heading for Derby

know nothing about football was to double your sins. Fortunately Andy was also a football fan (Leeds United) and his ability to swap chit-chat about Billy Bremner with the local bully boys often got us out of a bashing.

I didn't have any friends who weren't spotters. Not best friends, anyway. But it was surprising how many kids would take up spotting in order to become your friend. Declan Mulroney, for instance, a newcomer to the grammar from outside of Burton. Stigmatized by his Irish name and his sticky-out ears he was desperate to fit in. To this end I blackmailed him into ditching his stupid bus-spotting hobby and accompanying me on a trip to Manchester. But he was a good-natured kid and he didn't resent these conditions. I could never be sure, though, if he really liked spotting or whether it was just an impost on him. Whatever the case, we got on well together, and it was my turn to be sad when he moved on to yet another school only a few months later.

Horninglow Station

After it was closed in 1962, the dinky station at Horninglow became a transport café. The platforms were chipped at the edges and overgrown by grass, but inside the old booking hall lorry drivers could tuck into eggs 'n' bacon. The line itself remained open and the passing freights set forks jangling against tea mugs.

On 2 April 1966 it was curtains for the line too. Andy Parker and I went along with a banner we'd made. 'Up With Steam' it said on a white blanket nailed to two sticks. With the goofy optimism of youth, we held it up high and proud, but no one took much notice.

The signalman leaned on the window rail, cupping his cigarette to protect it from the steady drizzle. Eventually he received the bell and uncranked the gates across the road. A diesel shunter phut-phutted past us with a load of empty coal wagons. The *Burton Mail* photographer took a picture. And that was it. The signalman – depressed, redundant, nostalgic, who knows – locked the box and walked down the road to the pub.

Even in 1966 we knew that time was running out and

were always on the lookout for souvenirs, anything that could be unscrewed from its moorings and put away for posterity. There were so many signs left: Refreshment Room, Gentlemen, countless Trespassers Will Be Prosecuted signs, which didn't just have the warning, but included sections from the relevant acts, all cast in tiny quarter-inch-high letters. Such craftsmanship, such pedantry!

At Horninglow there was a cast-iron station nameplate. How it had survived so long I couldn't guess. Surely one of the lorry drivers with an eye for a quick buck would have jemmied it off its mount and sold it by now. But no one had, and there it was, a fabulous prize. With no one left to watch us, Andy and I set to work with a screwdriver from his dad's workbox. Prising and levering, pulling and jiggling and splintering wood, it

A pointless protest. Andy and I flourish our banner at Horninglow station in 1966

all seemed to take ages. But eventually the nameplate loosened and came off, the prize was in our hands.

Jubilant and breathless we took one end each and headed off in the direction of home. There was no argument about custody of the sign. Andy's parents would have had a fit if they'd found it in their garage, so our garden shed was ideal.

'Oi!' The bellow froze us in our tracks.

Turning round we saw a burly man in a vest striding after us. Should we run? Why the hell didn't we run I ask myself to this day. All I know is that we stood there like rabbits caught in a car's headlights.

'I'll take that,' he said sourly.

We gave it away. Just like that. And for all I know the bastard still has it. It probably graces the wall of his toolshed, admired by visitors. No doubt he notes the prices such relics fetch nowadays and prides himself on his 'investment'. I'm still as mad as hell, nearly thirty years later. This is my own personal Elgin Marbles. That sign should be up on my wall now. I should be glancing up at it while I write, filled by a warm glow of nostalgia for a damp spring day in my childhood.

Between 1966 and 1970 the railways were virtually stripped bare by trainspotters. Anything that could be unscrewed, unbolted or hacksawed away from its moorings could be taken away and hidden. There was a nationwide panic among trainspotters to save all those Trespassers Will Be Prosecuted signs, signal arms and clocks that had been in place for forty or fifty years.

The better off can afford £15,000 for a distinctive nameplate or £700 for the smokebox numberplate from a Scot, but the rest of us make do with a few buttons or a shedplate. Even sixties station names are much sought after now. All this I can understand, but a lot of it shades into nutcase territory. As with those fans who saved tissues a Beatle wiped his nose with, there are people with odd bits of metal which have the most obscure claims to a heritage: a sawn-off piece of handrail from the window at Carnforth signal box, a tinny seat supposedly from the driver's canteen at Crewe.

Collecting railway relics also brings some ethical dilemmas for trainspotters. For instance, can you count an engine as copped if you own its numberplate yet have never seen the complete loco in action? I'd be prepared to say no, though on trips round Crewe Works we would often count bits of engines, if they were big enough, such as a Britannia's boiler or the detached cabside. But where do you draw the line? That is the big debate. In schooldays there were always a few ethical rule-benders who stood by their astounding assertion that you could count pictures of engines without having seen the actual thing in real life. That was always a no-no with the main-stream. But as to whether you can count a numberplate, I have to admit to needing some moral guidance. After all, it is the number, and in the final analysis the number is what trainspotting is all about. Does it matter if it hasn't got an engine attached? It's all to do with ethics. Human spare-parts surgery is a straightforward debate in comparison with this one.

There was one small compensation. Strolling past Horninglow a few days later, I happened to glance in the dustbins by the station, and there was the nameplate off the signal box, dumped and unwanted. Without a moment's hesitation I grabbed it – all five feet of it – and scurried home. This time there was no ambush and the souvenir is still with us.

006 Bristol Temple Meads

Bristol Temple Meads has always been my favourite station. The castellated honey-coloured stone and the clock tower give it the look of a minster somewhere in the shires, and even now, nearly three decades after the end of steam, its vaulted roof encloses a classic kind of railway space; big and light and dusty, full of old smells and echoes of the past.

This is what stations were like before they were messed-up by designers in jazzy bow-ties. Bristol Temple Meads. I love the name – it rolls around the mouth like an English plum. I can't say it without thinking of freckled girls in thirties hats and small boys with fishing nets. An odd *frisson* runs through me each time I stop here. I find myself struggling to remember things that dance beyond the fringe of my memory. Perhaps I was a porter here in the thirties, or maybe the tea-trolley boy falling in love with a ringleted girl glimpsed through the window of a first-class compartment.

Bristol is the gateway to the West, the junction where the lines from Paddington and the North-East meet, and all those holidaymakers who still choose to travel by train get excited by the thought that they're halfway there. In steam days, Blackies from Manchester and Jubilees from Leeds were uncoupled from their trains and exchanged for something green and romantic, a Castle or a Hall with a polished brass nameplate.

The perspective of Temple Meads lends itself to mystery. The lines bend sharply away from the station and disappear under a cast-iron overbridge. On my first visit I could only stand on the platform and watch as the trains pulled out for Exeter, Plymouth and Penzance, my head full of ideas about a warm and seasidey land somewhere beyond.

Bristol was my first long-distance trainspotting trip; three hours from Burton. A ticket was beyond the limit of my 10s pocket money, but the pull was too strong to resist. My mum didn't earn a lot, but as an only child I had exclusive claim to whatever spare change there was and could always beg or charm an extra pound.

The great days of the GWR were over by the time I got there, but I wasn't interested in chasing ghost trains any more. I wanted to see engines at their best and was unashamedly looking for diesels now, for Warships and Westerns and Hymeks. I knew quite well it was these same diesels that had usurped the Castles and Halls, but

I wasn't as sad or indignant as I made out to my friends. I loved steam as much as they did, but I'd had my fill of derelict glory. This was my age and I could enjoy the Westerns and Warships in their prime. It was a waste of good spotting time to be too standoffish about dieselization. All the same, I was glad I was on my own. I didn't have to explain myself to anyone and I could enjoy it all in my own way.

With their maroon paintwork and beaky yellow noses the Warships were quite charming. And I loved the names: *Magpie*, *Benbow*, *Zambesi*, *Pegasus* and *Zephyr*. Steamers had always been named after dusty writers, small colonies or warmongers, and I hated the attendant values that were slyly advertised to trainspotters and passengers alike. Yes, the Warships were named after the same warships that upheld the British rule, but at least they were colourful and ambivalent and free of the smell of schoolbooks. (I grew to love some of those dusty writers in time, but it's worth noting that there were never any trains named after Jane Austen or George Eliot or the Brontës; the only woman worthy of railway attention was Boadicea, no doubt because she was half naked and drove a wild chariot.) There was an obvious symbolism to the new order: we didn't have much of an aristocracy or an Empire any more, so why did we need engines named after past glories? Kids were getting cocky and rebellious, and they didn't give a toss for old guys like Lord Kitchener or Clive of India.

The Western class diesels had a sharper, more sculptured profile, with windows that looked oddly like a big version of Yves St Laurent's specs. But what really charmed me was their maroon paintwork and the cast-iron name and numberplates. That was what we all loved so much about the Great Western; it was a railway Ruritania clinging to its own colours and traditions, living by its own quirky rules. Even the names were a last fling of defiance. Every one was prefixed with the word that had given the class its name – *Western Queen*, *Western*

Pathfinder, Western Stalwart – and which also seemed to be a last two-fingers up at the corporate ethos of British Railways.

As late as 1966, nearly twenty years after nationalization, British Railways was still struggling to impose its rule on the past. The problem wasn't confined to the Western Region (how could they stop the public calling it the Great Western?); the railways were really a loose alliance of small republics, each with its own identity and history. Drivers and stationmasters didn't think of themselves as British Railways staff at all, but rather as Somerset and Dorset men or Great Central men. It was a harmless tradition, and an honourable one, but the management despised it and were determined to squash it. They succeeded in the end, and the railways have never since had that special *esprit de corps*. There is still much loyalty between the staff, but a slick corporate ethos is a vastly different thing to company pride. No one has a job for life any more, and a railwayman's boss is no longer someone senior and experienced, but just as likely a fresh-faced young man from university. Grumbling was always part of the railwayman's life, but in the old days he knew who to yell at, and he could get things off his chest without risking his job.

Bristol's main depot, Bath Road, was entirely dieselized, and temptingly jam-packed with Warships and Westerns. I walked round there from the station and stood on the bridge to get as many cops as I could. But I never managed to bunk it. Security was too tight. Unlike the ramshackle sheds of the steam age, built before trainspotters existed, Bath Road had been purpose-built with unwelcome visitors anticipated. Even the cheekiest trainspotter couldn't have got past the well-sited front office and down the cleanly tiled stairs to the glorious-smelling diesel depot itself. Bath Road was a showcase and, in addition to the usual objections, trainspotters would have looked untidy there. But there was always someone who claimed to have cracked it.

Other spotters told me about a well-built lad with premature sideboards who dressed himself in a BR jacket and slipped easily through the company defences. It sounded like a splendid dodge, but I couldn't help wondering what would have happened if the foreman had handed him a job sheet and told him to take a Hymek out to pick up some empty wagons from the goods depot.

Still, if Bath Road was impossible, the sheds at Barrow Road were more spotter-friendly. And they still had steam. The depot was in its last days, so no one cared much whether kids wandered in or not. Mainly it was workaday freight engines, nothing I couldn't have seen on the lines around Burton. However, one or two GWR locos lingered on, still working (though they'd be in the breaker's yard within a year), but, as I'd expected, stripped of their plates.

I often wonder why my mum let me go so far at such a young age, considering how much she cherished me and the fact that we only had each other. But, knowing she'd only worry and grumble, I didn't always tell her the truth. I had no qualms about saying I was going ten miles to Derby when I had every intention of going two hundred miles in the opposite direction. If anything had ever gone wrong I dread to think what would have happened. My poor mum just wouldn't have known where I was. Britain was seemingly a safer place in the sixties. And it wasn't as if I was especially naïve – I knew all kinds of things could and did happen to kids on their own – but I think I must have believed I was an angel rushing in.

Even at the age of thirteen I was getting about more than my schoolmates, each trip taking me further and further away in ever-widening circles. I was the ripple in the pond, but who'd cast the stone? No one else in my class had ever gone as far as Leeds or Bristol, and certainly not on their own. They had their excuses of course – Andy had had enough of the so-called Great Western and Pipsqueak hated diesels more than any of us – but it didn't stop me showing off my Warship and Western cops to them. At morning break I could talk with authority about the quirkiness of the Warships and the clean lines of the Westerns. I knew they were jealous, but they turned their jealousy on its head and threatened to blackball me. It looked suspiciously like Whittaker was becoming a diesel-lover. Why all this enthusiasm for diesels when there was still steam worth going off to see?

Much as I enjoyed the camaraderie of trainspotting, I also cherished my solo status. Crewe, Derby and Snow Hill were shared experiences. But Bristol, like Leeds and Oxford, was something I wanted to keep to myself. I liked being on my own, but there was never any shortage of company, there was always someone to talk to. Most of the kids I met in Bristol were from odd little Western places like Tiverton, Westbury or Carmarthen, and they'd grown up in a totally different trainspotting culture. What was novelty and mesmeric for me was common as muck to them; they'd finished off their Warships and Hymeks twice over by the time they reached puberty. They couldn't see what I was so excited about.

If Bristol was exotic to me, I was just as exotic to the kids down there. Gritty, Northern, mysterious, I was also a sucker for flattery, happy to sit on a luggage trolley telling tales. 'Fetch us a cup of tea then,' I'd say. And as I sat there sipping and telling them about Peaks D1 to D10 I could see them going green around the gills. Burton was the only town where you regularly saw D1 to D10, since they were restricted to carrying coal to the local power stations. I saw them every day, but these kids would have to make it a major expedition, and even then they'd never get the set in one day. It wasn't only my intimate knowledge of Peaks and Bo-Bos I could impress them with. The younger ones had grown

Affectionately known as the Ford Anglia of the railways, a Hymek (no. 7009) leaves Paddington with a stopping train for Hereford in 1975

up on the front line of dieselization, they'd never even seen a steam engine . . .

My love affair with Bristol has lasted all this time. Yet apart from my walks to the sheds back in the 1960s, I've never been out of the station. My affection was based solely on what I'd seen from the train: the neat terraced houses, the red roofs of suburbia on the horizon, the gleaming wire of the Clifton suspension bridge, and mental pictures of the docks left over from reading *Treasure Island*.

I never even considered that the city could have another dimension, so the St Paul's riots in the eighties and the debate about the city's slums and underclass really shook me.

Temple Meads today is as grand as it always was, but there are signs of neglect at the edges. Apart from Birmingham or London, no town or city is busy enough nowadays to need fourteen platforms. But at Temple Meads they're rather stuck with them. They get used on odd occasions, but it's hardly worth keeping them spruce or providing refreshments for anyone caught out on a limb. The small tea and biscuits outpost which had its own slack regime and was, it seemed, maintained mostly for the benefit of trainspotters, is today boarded up and forlorn.

007 Waterloo Sunset

There were steam engines in London until the summer of 1967. It hardly fits in with the swinging sixties myth, but while The Flowerpot Men were inviting everyone to San Francisco and the London streets were perfumed with incense, the expresses from Waterloo were still steam-hauled. A mile from Carnaby Street, across the river, Waterloo was one of the last old-fashioned termini.

British Rail had just invented InterCity and were busy sploshing everything with corporate blue paint. They wanted us to think everything was set fair for the future, but the super modern image was betrayed by the old-fashioned sizzle of steam and the primeval smell of coal. I loved it, it was mutiny, a last stand against the boredom of dieselization.

I visited London several times that summer. With my ten bob pocket money and £1 from my paper round, I had enough. A child return to London was only 17/6 (there wasn't a half-fare ticket, so the clerk had to improvise by snipping an adult one in half diagonally) and the remaining money was enough for bus and Tube fares and something to eat. The fruit stalls in Soho were selling three peaches for two shillings, and that was an admirable lunch; liquid refreshment and wholesome vitamins all in one.

Waterloo was a wooden, brown and fascinating place, alive with the constant flutter of the indicator boards and the scurry of pigeons. It hadn't yet been sterilized and Dixonized and turned into the bland place it is today. Like Crewe and many other stations, Waterloo was a sprawling bazaar, full of flower stalls, tobacco kiosks and shoe-shining machines with their eccentrically whirling dusters.

The furniture of railway stations has changed drastically over the years. In the 1960s adults and children could find some eccentric amusements. My favourite was the foot-vibrating machine. Looking very similar to the scales you used to find outside chemist shops, there was a nasty shock in store for any Colonel Blink character who wanted to check their weight. You stood on its platform, put a shilling in the slot, and it vibrated your feet back to life. There was a delicious but slightly alarming loss of control. Or the sense of it at least. You felt as if your feet had been turned to a kind of goo and your legs were sliding away from under you, rather like the watch in Salvador Dali's painting.

Even more attractive, especially for the would-be pop stars (and which of us weren't?), were the booths, no bigger than a telephone box, in which you could cut your own record. On one occasion when I took my mum to London with me, we squashed ourselves in one for an impromptu recording session. While Mum sang a passable version of Ken Dodd's 'Tears', I spoilt it all by sniggering and making silly noises.

It was at Waterloo that Ian Allan, the patron saint of trainspotting, had the vision that would change the face of boyhood. In 1942, while working as a railway clerk, he invested all his savings and published the first ever *ABC* spotting book, a list of Southern Railways locos. Despite some initial opposition from the railway companies (it was halfway through the war and spy paranoia was rampant) the enterprise was a great success. Such a success that it seemed to be getting out of hand. 'Train craze sweeps the country!' yelled the *News Chronicle* in 1944.

Like most crazes, it was frowned on by older people. Quite apart from not understanding the game, the sight of other people's fun always rankles – doubly so if those people are youngsters. 'During school holidays as many as 200 boys at a time go trainspotting at Tamworth,' said a police inspector during the court appearance of two dozen Brummie lads up for trespassing on the tracks. (This event must have seeded itself in folklore. Even when I started spotting, twenty years later, the name of Tamworth was mentioned as a kind of cautionary totem.)

Quite apart from the dangers of trespassing (and railways have always been private property) what must have unnerved the authorities was the idea of two hundred young working-class people gathering in one place. The invasion and the trespass wasn't just physical either: these kids were trespassing on middle-class territory. A scholarly interest in railways had always been acceptable for gentlemen ever since Victorian times, but far from welcoming a wider audience, the old guard were horrified. These kids with their simple-minded 'trainspotting' threatened to bring the whole thing into disrepute.

Soon after the Tamworth rampage, to avoid being labelled as a Pied Piper for a ragamuffin bunch of trespassers, Ian Allan formed his eponymous Locospotters Club. Members received a badge (in de luxe chromium, 9d extra), a membership card, a pencil and a one-shilling voucher. You first had to sign your promise:

> I, the undersigned, do hereby make application to
> join the Ian Allan Locospotters Club and
> undertake on my word of honour if this application
> is accepted to keep the rule of the Club. I
> understand that if I break this rule in any way I
> cease to be a member and forfeit the right to wear
> the badge or take part in the Club's activities.

This effort satisfied the authorities, but I doubt if many club members felt that honour bound to keep a rule which would have destroyed half the fun of trainspotting. Some of the more timid spotters felt they ought to obey, but peer pressure always won the day. Quite how Ian Allan would have gone about getting the badge back off renegade members is unclear, though the more naïve were convinced that such misdemeanours would be found out. This would then entail some kind of public humiliation – badges ripped off blazers in full view of one's peers, banishment from trainspotting places, one's name mentioned in a Roll of Shame in one of the railway magazines.

Southern drivers were well aware that they had the honour of being the last men in Britain to drive steam-hauled expresses. They could still cling to the idea that train driving was an important job, and at the end of a trip to Bournemouth child-passengers would come and say goodbye before they had their week's holiday.

Unfortunately I never had quite enough money to go down to the south coast. But I did take the suburban lines out as far as Clapham Junction, where, in the summer of 1967, I couldn't help feeling sorry for southern trainspotters. With the West Country pacifics on the way out, they would soon have nothing left but crummy electric units, hundreds of them, all exactly the same. The South-East was infested with them already, and soon they'd be coupling up into 12-coach trains and pretending to be holiday expresses. The Southern Region had never had any diesels to speak of, only the humdrum Cromptons shedded at Hither Green, and they were too box-like to attract much admiration (though by 1994, as one of the last diesel classes, they were to enjoy a brief period of adulation from loco-starved spotters, but it was desperation rather than true romance).

The site of today's Nine Elms fruit and veg market was home to the last steam depot in London, also called Nine Elms. (Nine Elms, Old Oak Common, Cricklewood, Hither Green. Why did all London's railway places sound so misleadingly rural?) Here, right below the windows of council flats, West Country and Merchant Navy pacifics were polished and fired-up in readiness for their trips to Bournemouth and Weymouth. With their squared streamlining and distinctively spoked wheels, the West Country engines were one of the most popular classes. I'd seen my first one at Oxford in 1965, when it brought in the northbound Pines Express, and I'd been chasing them ever since. There was a romantic edge to collecting all those seaside-sounding sort of names like *Appledore*, *Lyme Regis* and *Clovelly*.

Nine Elms was a top-notch depot, yet they didn't seem too bothered about kids like me wandering around. British Rail despised these wonderful steam engines now, and couldn't wait to get rid of them. But the drivers and cleaners were still proud of them and of themselves; they wanted kids like me to see the twilight's last gleaming.

Things didn't always go so smoothly, though. I'd had

a few scares over the years, but none like I was destined to get later that summer.

Nine Elms and steamers apart, I'd always thought there was something a bit sinister about the Southern Region. It was something to do with all those electric trains and the almost casual footnote to Stewarts Lane in the 1965 *Locoshed Directory*: 'Caution, there are live rails in the shed yard.' Death would be instantaneous for the careless trainspotter. The name Stewarts Lane still brings on an instinctive touch of nausea. No, I didn't get electrified, but it was here that the railways lost their fascination in a sickening way.

Bunking Stewarts Lane sheds was quite easy (if you avoided the electrified rails, of course). There was a small gatehouse at the entrance, but I'd walked past without being nabbed. It seemed like a perfect bunk, really. It was on my way out that things went drastically wrong.

Like a spider waiting in his web, a fat Cockney jumped out of the gatehouse and grabbed me as I strolled past. His fingers looked like sausages, but they gripped like iron as he frogmarched me into his office. It was a sunny day, but he had a two-bar electric fire on full, and the place stank of armpits and sour milk. He took my spotting books off me, put them on a shelf, then sat and looked at me. I stood, frightened and contrite, while he toyed with the telephone dial. He was going to call the police, he said. Did I know what happened to trespassers? I would be put in a home with other delinquents.

My biggest crime seemed to be that, since he had not seen me go in, I must have walked across the main line to get into the sheds. Even I wasn't mad enough to walk across the busiest of railway lines in the country – eight or nine tracks, side by side and in constant use – and I told him so. But my protests fell on deaf ears. He obviously prided himself on his work and refused to believe that I could have escaped his eagle-eyed surveillance. I'd exposed a flaw in his security and he was determined to punish me for it.

He dialled a single 9 and let the dial spin back, watching me all the time. It was a nightmare. I begged him to let me go. I was beginning to cry. I wanted my mum. I wanted my home and my fireplace. (Years later, after reading the transcript of the tapes made by the Moors Murderers, my experience at Stewarts Lane returned to me. It seems flippant to place it in the same category, yet for a moment I knew the terror of being separated from the love and safety of home.) Finally I cracked. Panic-stricken at the idea of being parted from my mum, I did everything except get on my knees and beg. I cried and wailed and blubbered so loudly that he became embarrassed. His cruel game had got out of hand, he couldn't control the misery he had unleashed in me. Any railwayman passing would surely have intervened. Reluctantly, he handed my books back to me and pushed me out of the door, glad to be rid of me.

I was relieved, but I didn't feel triumphant. He had scared me too much for that. I was too naïve, too trusting in adult power to know that what he'd threatened was impossible. Dialling 999 to report a trespasser, for God's sake. Today's youngsters would have a solicitor on the case in minutes.

The name of Stewarts Lane haunted me for a long time afterwards. Ten years passed before I dared to go back, and only then because I didn't want to look foolish in front of my companion. I'd told the story many times over the years and it had become a bit of a joke. All the same, it was a heavy moment for me, since no one could really guess the genuine terror I'd felt that day.

But the fear quickly passed. The watchman's hut had gone. There was nothing left of it but some squares of tiled floor cracked open by thistles and dandelions. It was impossible to believe that some fat sadist had ever sat there in a chair and smirked at a small boy's terror.

Rooms with a view. Council flats overlooking the turntable at Nine Elms Depot in the heart of London

In fact, the whole area seemed so much smaller. I almost laughed with relief, then I saw two railwaymen coming off shift and fought the urge to bolt for it, but they merely nodded a greeting to us as we passed.

Waterloo has precious few charms now, no shoe-shining machine or pop-star booths. I've nothing against the Eurostar terminus, but it looks nothing like a station. Marketing wisdom insists that if railways are to compete they've got to look like airports, which is a sad comment on society. British society, that is. Over at the other end of the line the Gare du Nord still looks like a railway station, its form and its function happily in harmony. (Half close your eyes and you can still see the station as it was when wide-eyed Americans came to indulge their literary daydreams in the 1920s.) It smells of romance and history, but it's still a Eurostar terminus. So why does ours have to look so glassily boring?

So much effort is put into denial. Railways may have a future − but not as railways. Stations must look like airports, trains must look like aeroplanes, drivers must look like pilots (no walking down the platform with a billycan of tea). Even the ticket staff are redesigned as beaming hostesses and speak with robotic phrases that pass for 'customer care'. (How I wish the blind would flick up at Waterloo International tomorrow and a tooth-less Moore Mariott screech at the hapless passenger 'Next Eurostar's gone!') That's the kind of occasional, life-enhancing comedy I'm so scared of losing. Many would say it isn't even comedy at all, just a symptom of everything that was wrong with the railways; not a comedy that cheered passengers up, but rather made them weep with despair. There's a grain of truth in that, but British Rail's ideas for our future scare me more.

It's not that I'm stuck in some mythologized steam age, opposed to all change or progress on the railways. I'm fond of my memories, of course, but I'm all for going forward, too. Technology has undoubtedly improved rail travel in a host of ways (faster, cleaner, comfier), but at the same time a lot of what passes for progress and modernization is just cosmetic, less to do with the smooth running of the railway machine than the image of its employees, magically more efficient because of a fancy title and a white shirt with a name badge. The story changes so often: the railways that were recently held up as an example of Britain's Golden Age are now accused of being grossly inefficient, run by too-gentle gentlemen and staffed by surly Luddites who couldn't give a toss about passengers. This shameful rubbishing has been put about to show today's railways in a better light, but 'customers' certainly pay for all the 'added value' of computerized booking screens and sweet girls with walkie-talkies. There seems to be millions available to invest in computers and customer-care training days, but precious little to build new trains with.

008   The Black Cities of the North

We always envied those kids we met who came from Manchester and Liverpool. They'd been born lucky. What a wonderful trainspotting life they must have had – dozens of depots to bunk and houses with railways in the backyard. But they always seemed thinner, paler, and not as tall as the rest of us. They were so obviously poor, too. Why else would they have to wear their school blazers at the weekend? Yet however superior we might be inclined to feel, one look at their Ian Allan books was enough to knock us sideways; they were jam-packed with Scots and Jubilees, and Britannias like *Hereward the Wake* and *Coeur-de-Lion* which always evaded the rest of us.

'*Coeur-de-Lion?* That effing wreck? It's been shunting down Edge Hill yard all week long.'

Steam buffs ramble on about the grime and glory days of the sixties, but as a slightly Green 1990s person

I can't help but feel a ripple of guilt. The old puffers may have looked sweetly picturesque on the Somerset and Dorset or in the Derbyshire Dales; but, as far as I know, no one has ever gauged the effects of steam upon the health of the townsfolk of places like Lancashire and Yorkshire. These people lived out their whole lives under a speckled grey duvet of a sky, tutting at wash-day whites which never were and breathing in coaldust and sulphur.

Merseyside 1966

On my thirteenth birthday my mum presented me with a big blue fiver. The next weekend I set off to conquer Merseyside. This really would be a trip to tell the lads at school about.

First stop was Warrington Bank Quay and a quick bunk of the sheds there. Further up the line I changed at Wigan on to a steam-hauled local to Southport. A real treat as there weren't so many steam-hauled passos left by then, and the 3-coach train was empty enough for me to get close up behind the loco. With my head out of the window, I sniffed my way across Lancashire, from the smokiness of Wigan to the saltiness of Southport.

I had my head out of train windows for most of my teenage years and sported a working hairstyle remark-ably similar to a sweep's brush. I often wonder why I didn't get it knocked off. There were enough warnings – 'Do Not Lean Out Of The Window' it said on every door – and I couldn't help but be aware of the consequences. Morbidly, I tried to guess how I'd feel if my head got knocked off by a signal post and landed on the trackside: how long would I be conscious for? Long enough to be frightened? Would my optical nerves carry on working for a moment or two, so I would see a headless schoolboy leaning out of the rapidly vanishing train? I was fasci-nated and repelled by this horrible idea. But it didn't stop me tempting fate.

Southport sheds was ticked off as another successful bunk and the trip seemed to be going like clockwork – until I arrived in Liverpool at teatime. I was a weedy kind of kid and quite terrified by a stampede of burly men in whiffy lumberjack shirts on their way home from the docks. January teatimes are always gloomy and, intrepid as I thought myself, my thoughts turned to the safety of home. I was a long way from home and it was getting dark. Still, Birkenhead sheds were on my list and I wasn't going to pass up a chance of bunking them now I'd got this far.

8H was a huge place. In daylight I'd have been over-joyed – there must have been a hundred engines on shed – but the long rows of engines were barely illuminated and half the numbers were illegible. I began to feel over-whelmed by the unrelieved gloom. Frustrated and anxious to be home, I just gave up and hurried back to Lime Street to get my train to Crewe. It had been an epic trip, but I was so glad to sink into my seat on that rattling diesel train back to Derby.

One Sunday in Leeds

Travelling on Sundays was always dodgy. From a trainspotting point of view, the depots would be packed with engines returned to their home base for the week-ends, and, with few staff at work, bunking was easy and mighty satisfying. Getting there, though, could be a nightmare. Sunday trains were always slow and inevi-tably late. I still recall my horror one Sunday at Bristol when they gaily announced a delay to my homebound train – not ten minutes or half an hour, but three hours. And that wasn't really so unusual.

So I knew it was a bit risky going up to Leeds on a Sunday to bunk the four depots there. No one else wanted to come. They thought I was mad, but I didn't mind. I liked being on my own, and that's partly why I had so much success with my shed-bunking. No matter how quiet two or three kids might try to be, it simply defies the laws of nature. Alone, I found it much easier to slip through fences, tip-toe over crunchy slag, duck into the shadows or behind an engine whenever I was in danger of being nabbed.

My first stop was Holbeck, Leeds' main depot, still containing a fascinating mixture of steamers and diesels. Star cop of the day was *Clan McLeod*, one of a class of only ten, and the first one I'd seen. No one else in the gang had ever seen one. Flushed with success, I headed on to see what I could find in Leeds' other three depots, my next stop being Farnley Junction, a twenty-minute bus ride away.

You're probably wondering how a stranger to Leeds could find their way between all these depots, how they would know which bus to catch, and where to get off. Answer: I had the *Locomotive Shed Directory*, another essential book from Ian Allan. Though it was compiled by the very responsible-sounding Aidan L. F. Fuller FCA, and the publishers took great pains to stress the perils of trespassing, the pocket-sized book was for all intents and purposes the 'bunker's bible'.

Some sheds you could easily work out how to get to yourself. They were hard by the station, or you could see the curtain of smoke over nearby houses. But other sheds were up to an hour's walk away and Mr Fuller's well-researched data was vital. To get to Farnley Junction from Holbeck I had a choice of a 31, 32 or 47 bus, and on alighting I had only to 'walk along Royds Lane and bear right along a rough road just before the railway bridge'. I have that same 1965 shed directory in my collection of old books and I often browse through it and re-live those walks. It would be interesting to repeat some of them now. Although following the same instructions you would probably end up in the middle of a young executive estate, or in the paint section of a DIY superstore, with no earthly trace that a railway had ever existed in the vicinity. Most of the old sheds have been razed to the ground, though the odd one does survive, adapted for use as a garage or a warehouse.

By the time I'd bunked Stourton and Neville Hill and made my way back to Leeds station, the night was closing in. Waiting for my inevitably late train, I had plenty of time to think. The statistics of railway history are fascinating. I couldn't help wondering things like, how could there have ever been so much coal? Think of it, ten million trainloads of it, zillions and zillions of tons of black glittering coal. All cracked into useful pieces. I also frequently tried to work out how many sleepers there were on the whole of British railways. This involved extensive calculations. I knew there were 1500 sleepers per mile. This then had to be multiplied by the number of track miles. More surreal was the challenge to calculate how many clickety-clacks there'd been over the last century. And, was the clickety-clack that I heard the same as the clickety-clack further down the train? How could it be calculated? You'd have to multiply the number of wheels by the number of gaps in the track by the number of trains. We didn't have calculators then, so I tried to work it out in the back of my spotting book. I was a deep deep kid.

The Manchester Trips

By the end of 1967's flower power summer, steam was in retreat all over Britain, banished from the West and the East, from Scotland and from Tyneside. It had its last stand in the smoke-blackened cities of Liverpool, Leeds and Manchester, and in the Clinker Triangle between Bolton, Blackburn and Preston. That Christmas my mum bought me *The Decline of Steam*, a huge 'coffee table' book costing three guineas, full of black and white photographs of steam engines. There was no need for words, the grainy pictures said it all. We had some serious spotting left to do.

It was around this time that I first met Jinx. I'd known

him vaguely by sight as he lived in the same street, but he was older than me and went to the secondary modern, so our paths never crossed until I got a paper round at the same newsagent's as him. He asked me one day if I fancied going to a pop concert (Spencer Davis, The Hollies, Paul Jones and The Tremoloes – 17/6 including coach fare to Leicester) but it wasn't until we got talking on the coach home that I found out he was a trainspotter.

Usually summer is the season that people recall with fondness, even when a simple check of the weather records belies their memories of balmy days and herb-scented evenings. I'm the same with winters; mine were all sharp and frosty and quite delightful. In these mental home movies 8-Freights and Blackies struggle bravely through Peak District blizzards, slipping on glassy rails, scattering ice and sending clouds of grey smoke over a countryside which looks as cute as a Christmas card.

The winter of 67/68 was just like that. Jinx and I used to catch the train from Derby to Manchester to bunk some of the sheds spread around the city. We'd strike off early, with sandwiches and flasks of Heinz soup tucked into our tartan duffel bags. Our train was a two- or three-coach affair, yanked along by a plucky little Bo-Bo diesel. There may have been some minimal heat-ing seeping through into the cold compartments, but whatever you did to the star-shaped knob marked HEATING it never made any difference. The toilets were always iced-up, and giant pitchers of water were provided for flushing the pan. But the train got warmer as the journey progressed and then, with soup warming our insides and the hot air from under the seats blissfully wafting our flares, the journey became enjoyable. More than enjoyable. Rocking and rolling through the snow-covered hills and roaring tunnels of Derbyshire became a truly magic experience.

Trafford Park was the depot we'd cottoned on to first. On a coach trip to see Manchester United one Saturday (Jinx was the fan, I was easily swayed), with an hour to kill outside Old Trafford before the game, we'd caught the whiff of coal and steam. It didn't take long to track it down to the sheds just around the corner. Distracted by girls and pop music, we'd neglected trainspotting a bit, but this trip reawakened us, reminding us of what was still left and how soon it would be before it was gone for ever.

Forget the anorak myth. We were cool guys in 1967, bang up-to-date with the fashion of the time. (The spotter in short trousers and a school mac was already a thing of the past, as doomed as the steam engines themselves.) I had a chocolate and cream polo neck and a pair of hipsters with a thick leather belt. The check was so loud it wouldn't have disgraced an American tourist in Stratford. The shoes were fourth-form regulars, as even with the extra cash from my paper round I couldn't yet afford any Chelsea boots. I was aware of the discrepancy, but I kidded myself that hip footwear was hardly practical for scurrying over piles of coal and clinker.

Patricroft was our favourite depot. There were always many ways of approaching an MPD, officially and unofficially, but no spotter crossing the footbridge over the railway at Patricroft could fail to be excited by the smoky panorama that greeted him. Patricroft was always packed out. There were plenty of workaday locos on shed, but Patricroft had a slightly exotic touch and Britannias were regular visitors there.

Newton Heath was still one of the biggest and busiest sheds in the country. But it had a shameful corner, like many sheds at that time. A 'scrap-line' was where they kept locos that were not officially withdrawn, yet were too clapped-out to carry on. Britannia 70023 stood cold and lifeless at Newton Heath for months. (*Venus* on the scrap-line!) The depot staff didn't seem to mind us clambering around and posing for snapshots in the driver's seat. The rusting express loco was now just a big plaything for the kids. How could this be happening? we asked ourselves. The Britannias had been built only fifteen years before and were intended to be the pride and joy of British Railways. Was it possible that only a

Jinx beside an 8-Freight at Stockport sheds in 1967

year or so previously we'd seen *Venus* at Crewe station, sleek and green at the head of a Carlisle express? Even ordinary passengers thought they were getting a good deal when they saw one of these beauties at the head of their train. But now . . . What crazy economics were going on here?

Pop songs, especially those of the sixties, are inextricably tied up with my trainspotting memories. Without them, I could never have dated all these tales so accurately. Steamer Gates was 'The Last Time'; Crewe was 'Ticket to Ride'. 'Elusive Butterfly' recalls a trip to Doncaster, and 'Monday Monday' instantly brings to mind Sheffield (even though it was a Saturday). But it's always mystified me as to where the music came from. I didn't have a tranny and anyway there was no Radio One to listen to until the end of 1967. I like to think that the music was in the air, like the soundtrack to a film, yet I know that is impossible. My only explanation is that I memorized the tunes from *Top of the Pops* and hummed them to myself whenever there was nothing else going on.

Ten years later, when there were only diesels left, I sat on the stations at Taunton and Plymouth humming my way through a medley of seventies hits, and got mildly tipsy on the diesel fumes that drifted across from the waiting expresses. Sixties, seventies, eighties, the music has always been there. And whenever one of the old songs is played (usually on Radio Two) I'm immediately back in the past, in one particular place on one particular day, and I can smell the coal and the diesel and the dusty carriages.

009 Yesterday Has Gone: 1968 and the Last Days of Steam

August 1968. The month is etched on our memories. A group by the name of Cupid's Inspiration was shooting up the charts with 'Yesterday Has Gone'. And it was the month that steam engines were finally expelled from British Railways. We'd had years to get ready for it, but the 1968 Ian Allan *Combine* still came as a shock. It was so thin and insignificant. I remembered, still remember today, the first one my mum bought me, fat and shiny, with that petrol smell I associated with the adventure of books. But in the four years I'd been buying the *Combine* it had shed thousands of numbers. They'd already stopped issuing a separate steam book – it would have been derisory, no more than a flimsy pamphlet – and even the *Combine* wouldn't have been worth its 12/6 if Ian Allan hadn't resorted to padding it out with a twenty-page puff for the rose-tinted hi-tech future of the railways.

Not that steam fans cared. As far as they were concerned there was no future. It wasn't only their darling steam engines that were destined for history's dustbin, but the whole damn thing, that great smoky teenage playground: signal boxes, sidings, men in grubby jackets and crumpled caps, station porters, in fact, anything that made a noise or cast a shadow.

The future railway scene would be eerie and soundless: clanking signals would be replaced by winking lights; a million rattling wagonloads of freight would be transferred to the roads; and even the track itself was being welded into long continuous strips, so there wouldn't even be that clickety-clack clickety-clack any more.

If there had been any poets on the British Railways Board they might at least have let the lads enjoy one last glorious trainspotting summer, two more of those long hot months of pop and sandwiches and the smell of coal. But the holidays had hardly even started before steam was wiped out. Still, at least the weather was good. If the end had come in winter the engines would have limped off to the scrapyards veiled in drizzle and smog. As it was, they departed in carnival weather and the crowds came out to pay their respects.

Three names are inextricably linked with those final days of steam: Rose Grove, Lostock Hall and Carnforth. These depots were the last bastions of main-line steam and formed a 'Black Triangle' between Preston, Blackburn and Lancaster. This is where they all came, a steady stream of trainspotters desperate for a last glimpse. The railwaymen made them welcome too. There was no kicking ass now, no harsh words about trespassing. The visitors were even invited to help out and get to work with their rags and polish. British Rail may not have given a damn, they just wanted it over as quickly and quietly as possible, but the railwaymen and trainspotters were determined to make an occasion of it.

The trainspotting equivalent of the JFK question is 'Where were you on the last day of steam?' The faithful will be able to say they were somewhere in Lancashire, chasing every possible working, snapping every possible picture, drowning their sorrows in a Carnforth pub. They'd been hanging around for months, but there were so many people turning up at Carnforth in those last few days they had difficulty parking their cars.

I know where I was: I wasn't there. And I've never overcome that guilt. I had chased steam around the country for four years, as much as my pocket allowed, and I couldn't even make it a hundred miles to Lancashire to join in the wake. I dread having to explain myself one day, to my grandchildren, perhaps. I'll feel like a soldier too ashamed to admit I wasn't at Dunkirk. While the others were mooning around the sheds at Rose Grove and Carnforth, or chasing the last freights up to Carlisle, I was more interested in the discos at St Chad's church hall and shaking my hair to 'Jumpin' Jack Flash'.

If one of the gang had wanted to go, we'd probably all have made the effort. But no one did. Pipsqueak would have been too proud; he would have hated to see those 8-Freights and Blackies limping from one humble duty to another, leaking steam, covered with a blistered rash of limescale that no one could be bothered to clean off. Andy seemed to be more into football and had ambitions of managing his own team of juniors.

But there was a more sombre reason for our absence. Jinx's mum and dad were killed in a car crash, and it had thrown a shadow over all of us, especially Andy and me, because we'd been round at Jinx's drinking his dad's beer and dancing to Stones records when the police came with the news. It was a tragedy for Jinx, of course, but it made us all feel vulnerable too. Part of the joy of trainspotting was coming home to love and a hot meal, then clearing the table to sit down and do all the paperwork. I loved my mum, but I'd always taken her for granted too. The idea that she wouldn't be there was too awful to even think about. It made me newly timid, a little less adventurous.

So how can I write with any authority? Maybe I can't, but the end of steam is part of railway mythology, so well-documented in words and pictures, in film and sound recordings, that everyone knows the story. I'd already seen the neglect and resignation elsewhere. Those last days at Wolverhampton and Tyseley, and those trips to Manchester, had given me an ample preview of what it would be like.

I don't think I was the only one who didn't go. Old trainspotters *are* like old soldiers; they all claim a share of the glory. No one can disprove them now. But if there had been that many of them swarming around, the county of Lancashire would have sunk two inches further down.

Arguments have raged ever since about whether the end of steam was necessary. To schoolkids and socialists (but not those in government) it had the smell of a political fix. While hippies were high on pot, the establishment was high on modernization. They thought they had a vision, a wonderful future full of high-rise blocks, supermarkets and comprehensive schools. British Rail had invented InterCity and painted all its carriages blue and white in an early attempt at a corporate image. Steam engines had no place in this vision, they were too obviously mechanical and emitted embarrassing smells. Yet, as we'd seen first-hand in Manchester, some of the steamers were barely ten years old (the last was built in 1960), and they could have lasted another fifty years. Indeed, the original plan was to keep steam well into the 1970s. Even die-hard steam fans, though, accepted that steam engines had to go one day, but not so hastily and with such a disgraceful lack of gratitude. The wealth of the nation owed much to the invention of the steam engine and its century and a half of loyal service.

Dr Beeching – a name even now accompanied by an

oath and a spit – was an ICI chemist drafted in as chairman of the British Railways Board in 1962. His vision was to concentrate solely on InterCity and high-speed freight. To this end he chopped the railway network by a third, and if he'd had his own way there'd have been no railways west of Plymouth or north of Edinburgh. The size of the change and the scaling down of the business can be gauged from the fact that 18,000 steam engines could be replaced by a mere 5000 diesels and electrics. There's even a domino theory that the end of steam marked the end of our industrial society. Without steam engines to keep fuelled, the coal industry lost its best customer and much of its strength. The railwaymen and the miners had always stood shoulder to shoulder, a vast army of men who understood the vital chemistry of fire and water. But the bond of mutual dependence had been broken and the hum and clatter of industry would never be quite as cheerful.

The weekend of 10/11 August 1968 saw the famous '15-Guinea Special' powered from Merseyside to Carlisle by the one remaining Britannia, 70013 *Oliver Cromwell*. It cost £15.75, about two weeks' wages, for the privilege of travelling on the last-ever officially operated steam train. British Railways were certainly going to milk tearful trainspotters for their last penny, and there was no shortage of takers. I suspect that the thousands of people who stood at the lineside and watched it go by had a better view – it may have been only a few seconds, but it was somehow more dignified than being on the train, fighting for a space at one of the tiny windows.

For me, steam had only lasted four short years. A quarter of my life then, but only a tenth of it now. And yet, emotionally and spiritually, it's always been more than half. I still have recurring dreams of steam. I'm back in the sixties (or steam has been revived for some reason), walking across a bridge, when I hear a whistle. I jump up to see over the ironwork, and it's all there, the whole of my childhood, all my summer-holiday cops pasted on to a long and vivid collage: an Ozzie rattling past with a coal train, a Blackie coupling up to a train-load of mixed wagons, a faithful little Jinty shunting in the sidings. I've had this dream on and off for twenty-odd years, once a month at least. Recently, during one of our sadly infrequent drink-meets, I plucked up the courage to tell Andy Parker about these sentimental dreams, and to my surprise he confessed that it was exactly the same for him.

Carnforth 1995. I'm a quarter of a century too late, but there is still steam here. Steamtown sounds a bit Disneyfied, but it is a fitting memorial to those last smoky days. With health and safety at work to worry about, and a stack of EEC rules, we can never recapture the authentic gloominess and neglect of those sheds (they couldn't risk visitors crashing down into an inspection pit or falling headlong into an oil slick) but there's still lots to snag the senses: the smell, above all, and the hiss of steam and that ever-present sense of power at rest.

Carnforth is also famous as the location for one of the smokiest and best of railway films, *Brief Encounter*. It's hard to believe, looking round here today, that it was ever possible to shoot the film in such a location, never mind make it convincing. All that passion and betrayal and eroticism, the whisper of steam and the gathering thunder of expresses with the hint of that final *petit mort*. That happened here? It makes me wonder if any romance could be filmed at Milton Keynes Central or Birmingham New Street. Highly unlikely, and such a pity. Much is made of the eroticism of cars, but it's tacky schoolboy sexuality, obsessed with phallic symbolism and Desmond Morris colour codes. The railways could never offer blunt symbolism like that, but they have certainly provided the setting for romance and eroticism over the years.

010   Barry Scrapyard

The steam age had its elephants' graveyard in South Wales, in the Barry Docks scrapyard of Woodham Brothers. It was an eerie, windswept place. On sidings overgrown by grass and potholed by puddles, row upon row of dead and rusting steam engines waited for the men with the oxyacetylene torches. Not just a few engines, but over two hundred, parked buffer to buffer. For many of them it was a pauper's grave; West Country pacifics and Great Western Kings shared the same fate as the humblest freight engines. With their smokebox doors ajar you could see their guts were all the same, they were just old boilers cluttered up with limescaled pipes.

For nearly two decades, from 1968 until well into the 1980s when it was finally emptied and closed down, Woodham's scrapyard was an essential pilgrimage for trainspotters mourning the glories of steam. Not that there was any glory here, it was as joyless as any cemetery. Many steam fans kept well away from the place; better to stay at home with their memories, slides and a few mates with beer cans. What could possibly be the attraction of Barry? they demanded peevishly. Without the great tapestry of railway life hanging up behind them, and the men who fired them into life, these engines were nothing more than scrap metal. Better to get them cut up quickly instead of this lingering shame.

But we felt we had to go and have a look. For one thing there were engines at Barry which we'd never been privileged to see in action. Some of them, like the Kings, had been withdrawn before I even began trainspotting. It was a kind of necrophilia, I suppose, but I still wanted to add them to my list of cops. In years to come my grandchildren might say, 'You saw the Great Western Kings, didn't you, Grandad?', and there'd be no need to let them know that they had been orange with rust at the time, flaking away like cream crackers. I'd say that I'd not only seen them but I'd been up on the footplate, without mentioning, of course, the birds' nest in the chimney and the dog shit on the footplate. (How on earth did a dog get up there anyway?)

The 1968–69 period marked a watershed in our lives. Steam had gone and so had our childhoods. We'd all changed into cocky sixteen-year-olds and our thoughts were of girls and illicit beer-drinking as much as trains. Still, trainspotting wasn't something you could just throw aside like a game you'd got bored with. It had got into our blood. Even if we weren't so obsessed with collecting numbers, there were other things to do, grown-up sort of things like 'paying one's respects' to the past.

Six of us went on the Barry Trip in 1969. There was a sense of occasion, but that didn't stop us being daft. Like most teenagers, we were often cruel and thoughtless to each other, but at least we operated a rota system. Today it was Andy Parker's turn. While he'd been in the loo we'd knotted all the toggles of his parka to the strings of the luggage rack – a rotten trick which he discovered only as we were drawing into Cardiff station, where we had to change for the two-coach diesel down to Barry. Before he had time to undo them all, the guard was waving his green flag to send the train on to Swansea. Hearing the whistle, Andy flung the window open and shrieked: 'Emergency. Stop the train!'

We staggered round the platform hooting with laughter. Everyone stopped to watch, eager for some tragic spectacle – a heart attack, perhaps, or a leg trapped between the train and platform – so they were annoyed and disappointed when Andy stepped off, red-faced but otherwise healthy, with his coat.

The atmosphere on the train down to Barry was tense. It wasn't just the luggage-rack trick that had wound up Andy. He also suspected Jinx of stirring up mischief and division. I ought to have expected some trouble. Andy and Jinx had never been the best of friends: Andy supported Leeds and Jinx Man United, Andy liked Traffic and Atomic Rooster, Jinx liked The Hollies and Elvis Presley. It was volatile chemistry. With as much care as a society host, I'd always made sure that my different friends were kept in separate compartments. So I'd been uneasy when so many people expressed an interest in the Barry trip. Two or three was the optimum number, six people would have been anarchic at the best of times. With arch-rivals in the mix it was asking for trouble.

Once at Barry we calmed down a bit. This was no place for levity or bickering. Now and again, stumbling along the rusty gullies between the engines, we came face to face with other spotters. But there was no bonhomie, just a courteous nod and a typically British kind of shuffling past each other without any physical contact. Climbing up on the footplate we could sit on the driver's seat (if it hadn't been whipped as a souvenir) with our hands on the controls. But when you looked through the shattered windows it wasn't the line ahead from Waterloo you saw or the right-away signal from Liverpool Lime Street, but just rows of dead engines. This was reality. There'd be no more steamy days like those we'd known, no long summer holidays by the tracks waving to the drivers.

We were sad, but a kind of demob fever had crept up on us too. Let loose in this rusty playground we could climb up on to the cab roofs and walk along the top of the boiler, stick our heads down a chimney and shout four-letter words into the iron belly of the engines. Was this any way to behave? Maybe we'd spent so long in awe of the railways, been told off and chased off so many times, it was just a fun way of getting our own back.

As things turned out, we needn't have been in such a rush to get to Barry. Dai Woodham, the amiable scrap dealer who'd bought these locos and coralled them here, had no idea that he was to become the patron saint of preservation. If he'd got to work with his oxyacetylene torches as intended, the whole lot would have been gone within a year or so and Britain would be almost bereft

Barry Scrapyard, 1969: the gang poses on top of a knackered West Country pacific

of its working steam heritage. By leaving things be he gave many of the old trainspotters a reason for living.

Spotters were able to carry on with their pilgrimages to Barry for another twenty years. Amazingly, only two of those 215 engines were scrapped. All the others were sold off to some hastily convened band of preservationists or the odd spotting millionaire. For years we were bombarded by appeals from the 4247 Preservation Society, the MN Appeal, the Stanier 42968 Fund and a hundred others. Penny by penny, decimal coin by decimal coin, these ad hoc societies scraped up enough to save their precious engines from the bite of the oxyacetylene torch. Penny by penny is a fairly accurate description, since it took some of those societies twenty years to save up enough. It wasn't just a matter of towing away a crippled engine. There were still spirits in that wasteland (dead drivers and lost boys) and they couldn't be abandoned. They had to be guided back to the light somehow.

The last of the rusting wrecks didn't leave Barry until 1988, but it's as if they knew they'd be rescued one day, that their friends would never let them down. Rescued, reboilered, re-engined and repainted, every one of those wrecks is now in steam somewhere, spanking new and better looked after than ever before. We can congratulate ourselves that between us, with the accumulated spare change of a quarter of a century, we've preserved so much of the steam age in working order.

On the way back home we set fire to Andy's football paper while he was reading it, forcing him to shove the flaming sheets through the window. For all we cared it could have scarred him for life, turning him into some sad Phantom of the Opera figure, haunting the stations with his spotting book and his sandwich bag. At the least it could have started an embankment fire.

We certainly had some rip-roaring fun on our trips. Yet when I look back at railway magazines of the era, I'm impressed by their singular lack of humour. Not that you read *Railway World* for a laugh, but the language was so formal and correct. The oddest thing to my mind is that trainspotting, as such, was rarely mentioned – the magazines seemed to have loftier ideals, hence the emphasis on historical study and locomotive performance and timetabling. They couldn't quite shake off the lingering tradition that railways were something for Edwardian gentlemen to dabble in (and, after all, railway magazines had been around for half a century before trainspotting was invented).

Not that there was any lack of information for the trainspotter, it was just presented in a rather matter-of-fact way, without comment. Lads like Andy and Pipsqueak and myself bought the magazines for their pictures and their info, but they didn't talk our language. And their learned articles, however carefully researched, were rarely read by us or any other spotters we knew. We just weren't interested in long-winded technical waffle about 'LB&SCR Train Services of 1905' and suchlike.

This refusal to accept the average trainspotter as a flesh and blood youth is worth remarking on. As mentioned, the *Locoshed Directory* gave directions to every railway depot in the country. It was a bunker's bible, and every roving spotter had one in his pocket. It had been produced with bunkers in mind, and it made its profit from their pocket money, yet it had to go through the motions and stress that the book in no way sanctioned any trespassing or shed visits. It was as if it had been produced for purely academic purposes.

I believe all this formality and denial stood in inverse proportion to the real-life fun involved in spotting. Since Ian Allan had already been in trouble for encouraging trespassing and vandalism, he had to tread a thin line between running a profitable business by giving schoolboys what they wanted and being accused by the authorities of incitement to criminal trespass. He had to keep the peace with both factions, and it was not an enviable position.

The reminiscences in today's *Steam World* tend to back this up. All kinds of petty crimes and reckless antics are now coming to light, but the passage of time has given them a *Just William* quaintness. Such correspondence also lends support to my assertion that the trainspotting of the fifties and sixties was much more youthful and lighthearted compared with that today.

Back home in Burton, after the Barry trip, I got out the steam books I thought I'd never use again and began to mark off the engines I'd seen in the Woodham Brothers' yard. There were lots of cops: Castles and Halls from the Great Western, Battle of Britains and Merchant Navys from the Southern. I sat down with my ruler and lined them off, but I couldn't feel any of the joy I'd felt before. There was no satisfaction in it. It felt more like a duty that had to be done, that was all – my final audit of the steam age.

In common with every notable event that people can't quite bring themselves to believe, the end of steam was, and still is, surrounded by rumour. Conspiracy theorists will gladly draw your attention to discrepancies in the records. It's a fact that if the number of locos withdrawn from British Railways are checked against the total of locos scrapped and locos preserved, the figures don't add up. This is compelling evidence for the Strategic Reserve theorists, who claim the Government of the day decided it would be prudent to put by a fleet of steam engines in case of war or some national emergency where there was no oil. With diesels and electrics unworkable, we'd still have a viable railway system. It sounds like a logical idea, but no one's ever been able to prove it, and no government agency has ever admitted to it. No one is quite sure where all these engines are hidden, but the finger has often been pointed at Box in Wiltshire. There is evidence, not just from fanciful trainspotters, of some kind of secret subterranean fortress there. Certainly any-one seen in the area with a camera has been quickly tracked down and escorted away by police. And yet there's a considerable flaw in the Strategic Reserve theory. With hundreds of steamers already in private hands and in perfect working order, the government would surely be well placed to commandeer itself an emergency railway fleet if necessary.

The Seventies

011 An Itinerary of Despair: All-Line Railrover, 1973

For Andy and me, the All-Line Railrover was our last trip as trainspotting pals. It was an inspired but crazy idea born out of the desperation of our last teenage summer. We were both working – me in a crummy factory that made boiler jackets, Andy in the Parks Department of the town hall – but we still spent the evenings together, cruising the pubs and chip shops of Burton in Andy's battered Escort van. Nineteen seventy-three was a remarkable year for music. We'd had *Dark Side of the Moon*, *Transformer*, *Six Wives of Henry VIII*, and *Tubular Bells*, which seemed to thread those summer days like a silver ribbon.

British Rail still issued a separate timetable for each of its regions, so it meant buying all six before we could plan things in detail. It took weeks. If we were going to get our money's worth, every trip had to be carefully worked out with loops and figures-of-eight, so as little time as possible was wasted in doing the same lines twice. The word 'itinerary' cropped up constantly in our conversations with other people; one of us had found it in Roget's *Thesaurus* and it gave our jaunt an extra gravitas.

Every minute was vital too, which is why we took the 00.49 Burton–Bristol, the first train out of town. The last time we'd set off together on a spotting trip Burton station had been a grand Victorian building, proud with filigree and importance, coiled around with the thick brown aroma of history. But such smells were unwelcome. So they knocked the 1883 station down and replaced it with a 1970 Lego kit. Hard to believe it was the same place where we'd had so much fun. The waiting room with the leather benches and crackling coal fire was gone. All they'd left us with was a flimsy prefab with a drinks machine and an electric fire rigged to provide exactly thirty seconds of heat before switching itself off. The place had an air of meanness which no fine words about modernization could disguise. Across from the southbound platform the sausage and pie factory stood starkly against the skyline. The phrase 'dead of night' had a horribly ironic meaning for the truckloads of pigs who'd just been delivered. We could hear their panicked squeals ringing in the dark. A disturbing start to our holiday, but once on our way we tried to forget it.

> A star has followed our train to Bristol
> Playing peek-a-boo behind the trees.

I can't really believe I wrote that in my notebook, and I only include it now in the name of total frankness. The early seventies were still tinted with hippy ideals. We'd all been corrupted by Tolkien, and grown men could be heard talking quite seriously about elves and talking trees. I wouldn't be surprised if we secretly saw ourselves as brave hobbits setting off on some wonderful quest. We were still trainspotting (I have the numbers written down), but there was another, more spiritual dimension to this odyssey.

Neither of us said as much, but I'm sure we both suspected it might be our last railway trip together. Girlfriends and jobs had edged into our lives in the years since the death of steam, but we'd managed to contain the changes and keep some independence. We were kidding ourselves, though. In the past couple of months adulthood had caught up with a vengeance.

Andy had just split up with his girlfriend. Fussy about his women at the best of times, he thought he'd hit the romantic jackpot when he met Lynn. She had crinkled hippy hair and loved books and poetry – just the girl he'd been searching for all his life. Now she'd slipped from his grasp and he was deeply depressed. To make it worse, I was on a high. I'd been told by a married woman (all of nineteen years old) that she was madly in love with me. For the first time in my life I was on a real promise, even if I now had to wait a week for it.

I stared out of the window at the shadows and the colour signals which blinked from green back to red as the train rattled past. Whoever coined all that stuff about love and hearts was way off course: the guts was where it hurt. Despite the ache, I couldn't help smiling at the delights in store. Andy, meanwhile, was trying to lose himself in *Watership Down*, the latest tome (in 1973 we called all books tomes), but he kept catching my eye in the reflection and, having taken so much flak in the past, immediately thought I was laughing at him and his rabbit book.

'What's so bloody funny all of a sudden?'

I was bursting to tell someone. 'I met this girl last week. Well, I didn't exactly meet her, I knew her already. She fancies me so much she can't keep her hands off.'

'Yeah . . .' Andy had heard enough of my tales before, but when I told him who it was he went crazy. 'Jean? She's bloody married.'

'That's not her fault.'

'Colin's going to slay you down!' said Andy, as gleeful as a fire-and-brimstone preacher.

I repeated everything Jean had told me: how boring Colin was and how he left her on her own too much. Andy didn't give a hoot. The whole thing was immoral and despicable, but I was sure he just hated to see me happy. The week was off to a bad start.

After a doze, we arrived in Bristol as the sun cracked the slate-grey skies over Temple Meads station. Our first stop was the buffet. Bristol had an all-night one (there were still a few of them left then) and I was fascinated by the kind of people they attracted: an exotic mix of nutters, winos, trainspotters, insomniacs and kids recovering from all-night parties.

Weston-super-Mare was our first stop. We'd been thinking of a quiet stroll on a deserted beach before the plebs arrived with their kids. Andy had visions of beach-combing, picking up shells that had somehow been washed ashore from far away Sri Lanka. There was plenty to pick up, as it happened, but we'd have needed industrial gloves to do it. A canary-yellow bulldozer rumbled up and down the sands, trailed by half a dozen binmen stuffing empty Tango tins and ice-cream wrappers into black bags.

Disgusted and muttering about conservation, we hur-ried back to the station. Our next train took us all the way into Cornwall, to Liskeard where we changed for the two-coach diesel down the branchline to Looe. By this time we were starting to bicker. I'd been content to bring a small khaki knapsack with a spare pair of Y-fronts, my notebooks and a packet of fags in it, but Andy had decided to travel with a huge tube-framed contraption. It was a constant source of embarrassment; every time we got on or off a train he'd be knocking the spectacles off a pensioner's nose, poking some toddler in the eye or, even more dangerously, sliding one of the protruding poles against the buttocks of some hard-faced labourer.

We eventually arrived in Penzance at 18.18. Having had no more than crisps so far, we were desperate for some decent nosh. Choice was no problem. We simply followed our noses to whichever chip shop was respon-sible for the tasty smells that hit us as soon as we walked out of the station. Hurrying down to the beach with our hot parcels, we spread them out within view of St Michael's Mount, and tucked in. Our fish 'n' chip supper was a paragon of its kind; good fresh cod and fluffy chips stained with vinegar, all washed down with a bottle of Bulmer's cider.

I have some snaps of us on the beach there. We cer-tainly don't look like trainspotters. Our hair is long and uncombed and we're sitting, fags dangling, surrounded by empty cider bottles. We look like stragglers from some hippy convoy of old buses. Today we'd certainly be questioned by the police, our claim to be trainspotters met with a sneer and the steely glint of handcuffs.

At 21.30 we were on our way again, dozing away the 325 miles to Paddington. We rushed from there to Liverpool Street, snatched a 'Continental' breakfast, and boarded the train to Norwich. From there we looped back to London via Ely and Cambridge, thus taking in, at a fairly leisurely pace, two cathedrals and a university in a few hours.

Supper in the King's Cross buffet was a disaster. My steak and kidney pie was so flabby that the contents fell out on to the tray when I picked it up, scalding my hands and splattering gravy all over Andy's *Watership Down*. The chocolate I'd bought for afters had suffered so much in the summer heat that gobbets of brown leaked on to my trousers as soon as I unwrapped the silver paper. In the end I had to buy three bags of cheese 'n' onion. Good old crisps, you can always rely on them in an emergency.

Those were the days of rattling and unhurried overnighters, when you could get from London to Aberdeen without having to fork out for a sleeper. But I have to admit that it was often hell. The 20.00 King's Cross–Aberdeen should have been an epic voyage, but it turned out to be a club outing for all our most-hated travelling companions: nattering women, bawling babies, drunken soldiers playing poker in the gangways. At least we'd been early and got a seat. But how could we sleep? Answer: we didn't. We stared out of the window at the blackened countryside and wished death and dumbness on our fellow passengers. But fatigue had its way in the end, and after Newcastle we dozed, cradling our heads on the table. When we awoke the carriage was quiet and half empty, but we were almost in Aberdeen by then. We caught up on some sleep on the rattling bog unit to Inverness. I'd wanted to see Scotland so much, but I was just too tired to stay awake.

What was really getting on my nerves – apart from his rucksack – was Andy's constant harping on about the glories of nature. We couldn't pass a pine tree or a duck pond without some comment about how lucky we were to be alive. I knew he was just trying to soften the blow of being jilted, but I didn't have much sympathy. I'd rather he got mad and chucked lightbulbs out of the window, anything but this 'we're all pawns of a higher destiny' crap. To avoid being his nodding dog, I deliberately took up a contrary stance, pooh-poohing the rural idyll and thinking up a defence for every factory and eyesore community we passed. To me it was a revival of our old LNER/Great Western rivalry, a fun way to pass the time, but Andy took it all dead seriously and despised me for my flippancy.

Still, the rows were quickly forgotten whenever there was something to see. The train from Inverness to the Kyle of Lochalsh was intended to be one of the highlights of the trip, a sedate 30 m.p.h. cruise along what is allegedly the most scenic railway in the country. Andy was overjoyed by the hills, purple with heather, the streams of liquid silver, and isolated stations where no one got on or off. I let him off a ribbing this time. I was half asleep anyway, so it all passed like a kind of pleasant dream. At least we got to see the Isle of Skye, even if the rain came down in sheets. My abiding memory is of us crammed in the shelter of a phone box trying to get our sodden cigarettes to light.

We'd gone nearly a whole day without trainspotting. There'd been a few Bo-Bos in the shed at Inverness, two of which were chuntering away at the head of our train, but that was all. You don't go on these scenic lines for the trainspotting. It's mostly single track and there are no sidings or depots. In fact, to see another train so far out would be as incongruous as spotting a milk float in the middle of the savannah.

On the way back to Inverness we were joined at our table by two Glaswegians, not just any old Glaswegians but loud and angry ones. They'd been hoping to return home from the bottom end of Skye, crossing on the ferry to Oban and making a simple trip back to Glasgow. But they'd missed the boat and had to hitch-hike to the top of Skye, catch this train and return home via Inverness. Another complication was that they hadn't got any tickets. They had been able to afford a bottle of Whyte & MacKay, however, which they pressed us to share with drunken generosity. We sipped gingerly, anxious not to offend, but reluctant to exchange spittle.

'What'll you do when the ticket inspector comes?' I asked when I learned of their ticketlessness.

One of them growled, 'I'll fucking slay the bastard', and rained a torrent of karate blows on the table to make his point. The whisky bottle danced dangerously and the other one made a grab for it before it fell.

And here was the ticket inspector now, coming along the train, good-naturedly clipping tickets and chatting to the passengers. Should I warn him that Nemesis was on an awayday? The hardest of the Glaswegians glared at the poor man with concentrated hatred.

'This is ma fucking homeland, man, and the guy's telling me I can't go how I please? One word of English law and I'm going to put him in a coffin.'

Andy wanted us to move to another seat, but I wouldn't. I despised him for his snobbery. This was exactly the kind of adventure I wanted, the chance to sit and talk with nutters and thugs, not go all gooey about the mountains and lochs. Nevertheless, I prayed that the guy was just joking. I didn't know what I'd do if things started getting rough. At the same time I had this mad fantasy that if I somehow saved the hapless inspector from a slaying I'd be lionized in the popular press and rewarded by British Rail with a go-anywhere ticket for the rest of my days.

Suddenly one of the men got up and disappeared further up the train. The other seemed to fell asleep just ten seconds before the inspector arrived. We watched in horror as the inspector shook and poked him, convinced that the Jock would leap up and snap the poor man's neck with a horny fist, or smash his lovely British Rail hat with the empty whisky bottle. But no, the Jock's coma seemed so deep that waking him was impossible.

'He's been drinking,' I said helpfully.

The inspector shrugged and moved on, much to our relief. I expected the Scotsman to wake up straight away now that danger had passed, but he carried on sleeping.

At Inverness we had a supper of pie 'n' chips and a couple of pints of Tartan before boarding the overnight to Glasgow. We saw our two friends from the Skye train, but luckily they didn't see us. We expected a decent night's sleep, but this train too seemed to be an excursion for rowing Glaswegians, and a couple in the next compartment decided they were going to kill each other, but not before they'd each made a hit-list of all the relatives who were to blame for everything.

'I am telling ya, ya drunken git, that if ya dad looks at our Gina again like that I'll stick him wi his own breadknife.'

Glasgow Queen Street, Carlisle, London, Brighton, London, Swansea, Reading, Exeter. The signs flashed past our window in a blur. When we got back to Burton we'd be boasting that we'd been to all these places, but could furnish precious few details as proof. I was still doing my best to cheer Andy up with a clumsy 'plenty of fish in the sea' pep talk. There were dozens of slender hippy girls at Burton's 76 Club, I reminded him. He'd easily find a replacement for Lynn. But he didn't want to know. On top of that, he was getting irritated by my expectant smirk, which got harder to suppress as the end of the week got nearer. Why should I be so happy when he was so blue?

On day five we were back in Devon again, but this time the rain was slamming in off the sea as we approached Dawlish, leaving tiny gems of salt stuck to the glass. We were warm and dry, but Andy insisted we stuck to our plan to get off. He believed the more you got bashed by the elements, the closer to nature you felt. There was a certain gung-ho madness to tripping along the beach in the pelting rain, but we got so sodden and bedraggled that the layered soles of my shoes peeled off one by one. With no way of fixing them back, I'd have been banjaxed if I hadn't got a spare pair of plimsolls in my rucksack. What had started as a laugh now left me sitting in a café looking like a down-and-out, and the person to blame was sitting next to me sipping coffee.

This was the pits, the lower depths of friendship. Our eight years of trainspotting camaraderie were well forgotten. We were lovesick, unwashed, hungry, dog-tired and we hated each other's guts. If we'd had the cash or the credit cards (this was 1973 remember) we might have stopped off at a bed and breakfast, had a bath and a meal and a good sleep then started afresh. As it was, trains could go to hell. All we both wanted to do was to get home and sort out our lives.

Despite our personal problems it had been a memorable trip, and worth writing about. We'd both kept diaries, and when, a few months later, I got a typewriter for my birthday I set about sending off accounts to newspapers and magazines. Quite naïve about the ways of journalism, I thought talent would be enough to get me published. So I was hurt and puzzled when my five-thousand-word travelogues were returned with curt rejection slips. Slowly I learned the value of conciseness, and after each knock-back, I got a bit less hurt and did a bit more cutting. The whole odyssey was gradually wittled down, until, four years later, I managed to sell an eight-hundred-word version to the *Observer*.

012   Highland Flings: Women and Trainspotting

Railway excursions, once a vital part of British life, are now virtually extinct. The very idea sounds old-fashioned, unearthed from the same dusty trunk of nostalgia as charabancs and grocers in long aprons. Hard to believe then, that 'Merrymakers' (named when marketing men still had a sense of humour, or had just returned from the pub) ran from the Midlands every weekend as recently as 1973. As well as the seaside trips and 'London Shoppers' there were a variety of high-brow choices: Haworth for the Brontë Museum, Canterbury for the cathedral, Edinburgh for the festival. But it wasn't only normal people the Merrymakers appealed to. They were perfect for trainspotters who wanted to go a long way on the cheap.

For those of us south of Derby, Scotland was a tantalizing prospect. In Burton we were lucky enough to see locos from Bristol, London and East Anglia, but there was next to no chance of seeing anything from Inverness or Aberdeen. If you inspected anyone's spotting books, the yawning gaps were always the Scottish locos. Going Caledonian wasn't a whim, it always became necessary sooner or later if you were going to stand any chance of finishing off your classes.

We'd got our Edinburgh tickets back in June. Jinx and Aidie Parker (kid brother of Andy) were planning to use the Merrymaker as a cheap way of doing a Scottish bash, and that had been my intention originally. But I had a different set of priorities now. It wasn't trains I was thinking of. A day trip seemed like a good way of getting a rest from all the hassle I'd detonated with my extra-marital affair.

Not many husbands would consent to a rival taking their wife to Edinburgh for the day, but I was full of youthful arrogance and just took it for granted. Jean and I were in love. Why shouldn't we have a day trip? But I had lied shamefully too. Colin had pleaded with me to end the affair, and I told him I needed time alone with Jean so I could break it off gently and urge her to return to him. Colin was so desperate to have his wife back he'd go along with any suggestion. (Many years afterwards I realized how tolerant Colin had been; anyone else with my cheek would have been met by a gang of in-laws after closing time and taught a bloody good lesson.)

Colin looked a lot like the stereotypical trainspotter – harmless, bespectacled and anoraked – but he was, in fact, a model aeroplane nut. His marital strife was all down to this hobby. If he'd spent more time with Jean instead of glueing bits of balsa wood together she probably wouldn't have strayed. How ironic that when she did, it was with a trainspotter (even if he did wear a purple velvet jacket and two-tone shoes). To give Colin his due, he was prepared to sacrifice his hobby to save his marriage, and to this end he burnt all his precious planes in the back garden. The neighbours watched with open mouths as the flames licked up from what looked like a scale model of *Apocalypse Now*. It was a great spectacle and a grand gesture, but a mite too late to mend the neglect.

The Edinburgh Merrymaker kicked off at 5 a.m. Colin came to the station with us, in the forlorn hope that Jean would give him a farewell peck. He waved to her as the train pulled out, but she ignored him, gazing out of the opposite window and feigning interest in the coal depot. I felt awkward and guilty at seeing him ignored, so I waved him a cheery farewell. He was about to flash the V-sign in reply, but Jean turned just then, and he managed to remember his promise to be the world's most gentle and amiable husband.

While Jinx and Aidie jumped around to catch the train numbers at Derby and Sheffield, Jean and I sat and cuddled, relishing every minute of our time together. We didn't care a toss about Colin (we'd forgotten him already), but we felt a bit self-conscious in front of Jinx and Aidie. To be fair, they took it quite well. It had been meant as a boys-only trainspotting jaunt, after all, and no one was expected to turn up with a woman. It just wasn't the done thing. Not that Jinx and Aidie were rude, but our lovey-dovey behaviour obviously made them uncomfortable. Guilt was part of it. What if Jinx's wife had found out? Wives and girlfriends may be happy for their fellas to go off trainspotting, but it's on the understanding that there are no women around. Even if the pursuit of train numbers baffles them, at least they can relax in the knowledge that it's free from temptation. But if Jinx's wife had known that Jean had come with us there'd have been hell to pay.

One of the great subplots of the trainspotter myth is his abysmal failure with women. There are no female trainspotters, that's the problem. In thirty years of trainspotting, I've come across only half a dozen. The only one I recall with any clarity was at Crewe in 1965, a pre-pubescent tomboy dressed in green jeans and a patched school blazer. With her sexless figure and the patina of smoke and chocolate that smeared her face, she blended well into the male territory. There may have been some mild teasing from the other lads, but not much, because her brother looked like a mean bugger. And in any case, she knew her stuff and had a spotting book of her own with an enviable score of Scots, Jubilees and Britannias underlined in red. I remember being allowed to look at it briefly and feeling madly jealous. She came from some poorer district of Liverpool, so it was quite natural for her to have all those top-class locos whistling by the bottom of her street.

While modern women take charge in the boardroom or form their own rugby teams, none has demanded acceptance in the world of trainspotting. Women seem happy enough to be involved with the social and cultural values of preservation, but not the day-to-day paperwork of recording numbers. Alone at the end of the platform, notebook in hand, the trainspotter ploughs a lonely furrow. For any spotter who hasn't got a girlfriend, dating agencies are one answer. Dateline are regular advertisers in the railway magazines (but to be fair to trainspotters, wherever there are men there is always a market, and most other hobby magazines are good territory). These are men who know all about diesel transmissions and modern signalling, so they have great faith in technology – why rely on fate in the age of the microchip? They fill in their questionnaires with great confidence. But if finding a date for them is too much for the computer, readers of *Steam World* can always send off for introductions to 'Attractive Filipino Ladies'. Grateful to escape Third World poverty and willing to please, who better to trail behind hubby carrying the camera tripod and the Tupperware box full of sandwiches?

In 1993 there was an almighty rumpus when the *Sunday Times* Culture section ran a cover feature entitled 'Trainspotters – A National Joke?' It touched a raw nerve amongst the fraternity, who protested fiercely, and with some justification, against yet another re-run of the same old jokes. But what hurt their male pride most was the accusation that trainspotters could never hope to attract a girlfriend. In the letters of protest which flooded in, much was made of wives and girlfriends. One spotter from Lancashire even claimed to have half of the local hospital nurses in his harem: 'Lack of girlfriends? I get my "exercise" with a staff nurse from Blackburn and a casualty sister from Manchester!', which was a trifle exaggerated perhaps, but still, the newspaper's claim was an unfair jibe. It has its roots in a one-off joke made some time in the mid-eighties which had lodged itself in some editor's head and has subsequently been endlessly recycled by copy-cat journalists. Now, with the *Sunday Times* having put its weight behind the joke, what hope was there to rebut the stereotype? It had become part of our folklore.

But back in 1973, we were due in Edinburgh about lunchtime. The trip was long and arduous, even for seasoned spotters, and sleep had crept up on us all before we got to Newcastle. A short doze, but by the time we arrived at Waverley station the four of us were tangled up in an indecent knot, legs akimbo, clothes disarranged. As I opened my eyes I was sure I caught one of them getting an unofficial eyeful.

Tumbling out on to the platform along with a motley collection of shoppers, festival-goers and trainspotters, we adjusted our dress and arranged to meet up at tea-time. Glad as I was to have the day alone with Jean, I couldn't help feeling a twinge of envy as Jinx and Aidie set off to bunk the sheds at Haymarket and Polmadie. We'd come all this way, and it was such a golden opportunity. Didn't I have those same gaps in my book too? After ten years spotting I needed only eight out of the five hundred Brush diesels scattered throughout Britain. And five of those were Scottish, shedded at Haymarket. I might never have the chance again. I'm sure if I'd suggested a bunk of Haymarket sheds to Jean she'd have agreed, as anything would have been romantic just then. But how could I even think of exploiting her loyalty in such a way? Besides, it would have been really unfair on Jinx and Aidie, who must have been glad of a rest from the sound of kissing.

Nevertheless, the weather was perfect and, for a few hours, we managed to pretend that the world loved us as it should. But by six o'clock we were on our way home again. Jean was dog-tired and had nodded off in my arms by the time we got to Carlisle. I sat and listened as Jinx and Aidie compared notes and, with Jean asleep, I felt alone and excluded. Looking on as they slapped their rulers across the shiny pages of their *ABC*s and transferred all their cops, I really envied them the old satisfaction. I asked Jinx for a glance at his book and, holding it in my free hand, flicked through it. My gasp of annoyance made Jean jump in her sleep. They'd seen four, *four*, of the eight Brush I needed at Haymarket. Jinx and Aidie were highly amused by this. It had served me right, they thought, for deserting the brotherhood for the sake of a bit of nookey.

We got back to Burton about half-past midnight to find Colin waiting for us on the platform. He looked grim and determined, and I guess we must have looked a bit too happy, considering I was supposed to have cooled off the affair by then. Ignoring me, he grabbed Jean's arm and escorted her away. Had he guessed I'd been lying? I thought I was never going to see her again and felt quite devastated. If only I'd had the simple pleasure of going home to mark off my numbers.

013   Whoa! I'm Going to Lostwithiel: Western Railrover, 1975

Nineteen seventy-four was a year in hell. And 1975 didn't hold much hope of being any better. Jean had long gone back to her husband – we'd never stood a chance against the combined forces of in-laws and nosey neighbours – and even after a year I was still upset. Andy, in the meantime, had made it up with Lynn and they'd nested down in a tiny flat above a handbag shop. Not that I cared a toss for his well-being. I still couldn't get over how, after all those years trainspotting together, he could grass me up when I was having so much fun. To add insult to injury, he insisted that it had been for my own good.

All my dole money went on heavy Penguins. Sartre, Camus and Hermann Hesse were hardly the stuff to cheer me up. I was the Steppenwolf and the Outsider rolled into one, with a dose of Sartre's nausea thrown in to keep my nose up against life's toilet bowl. I prayed for someone to knock on the door – like Jinx did one day in June – and ask me if I fancied going on a trainspotting jaunt. Good old Jinx! He'd stood by me when the chips were down, offering Jean and I sanctuary from small-town gossips, fibbing for us when necessary. I owed him for that and happily agreed to go on a week's Western railrover in July.

Popping into town to stock up on notebooks and biros, I had a renewed spring in my step. My mum, for one, was pleased to see the old me resurface. She had been worried about my long face. Back home, I put all the miserable existentialist crap away in the bookcase and sat down with the latest *Railway Magazine* in order to catch up on what I'd missed.

Jinx's loyalty to the railways had never wavered. The end of steam had never bothered him that much, and he found plenty of interest in the seventies diesel scene. Not only that, he was on the team now, with a proper railwayman's hat, a whistle and a job as a guard. I had my own ambitions, and my sights were set firmly on London, but I couldn't help feeling envious. Sitting in a guard's van sounded like the perfect laid-back job to me – frowsting by the stove in winter, contemplating life from the little balcony in summer – not to mention its ultimate perk for trainspotters: all your rail travel for next to nothing. If I hadn't had that bee in my bonnet about 'making it' I'd have been happy to be one of Jinx's colleagues.

It looked like being a great summer ('Whoa! I'm going to Barbados' sang Typically Tropical) and it felt like the right thing to do, to be heading west again to see some of those snazzy Western diesels while they were still around.

It was only seven years since the end of steam, yet we knew that diesels were now under threat. Strictly speaking, diesels had been intended as a stop-gap between steam and full electrification. Many of the diesel classes had been built in a rush; they were nearly all prototypes, barely tested by the rigours of everyday service. Steam had been developed over a century and all the drivers were used to it – diesels were another matter. British Rail had commissioned dozens of classes, some successful, others not, some loved by drivers, others hated. The Westerns and Warships were good runners, no doubt about that, but being hydraulics they were non-standard: the majority of railwaymen knew neither how to drive them nor how to service them. Consequently these engines didn't fit into the grand British Rail scheme. Some diesels did survive another twenty years – testament to their design, but also to the fact that BR just couldn't raise the investment necessary to carry on with its ambitious electrification programme.

When we set off on the Friday night I felt as if I was beginning a new life, and it didn't take long for the old sense of fun to re-emerge. Sometimes, with hapless passengers yanking the communication cord because they'd got the wrong train, or the woman in the buffet telling us off for stirring our tea too fast and splashing the counter, the railways seemed like a 24-hour comedy act. And that was just at Birmingham. We had a whole week's trainspotting and sniggering to look forward to.

Warships and Hymeks had gone in 1972, and the

1008 *Western Pioneer* in Sonning Cutting on its way down to the West Country, 1974

Westerns were gradually being usurped by Class 50s as boring as vacuum cleaners by comparison (hence the nickname Hoovers). Jinx hated them and cursed 'Shit English Electric!' whenever one came along, especially when he'd spent ten minutes setting up his tripod and camera in the hope of a Western. But I refused to get riled. Taking sides was a waste of time. I was there for the Westerns, true, but I could find my pleasure just as easily with the incidentals; smoking a meditative cigarette and drinking a cup of tea in the Exeter buffet, or marking up my books while sitting in the sun on a cute Cornish station shadowed by yellowed palms.

Our trip to Barnstaple behind Bo-Bo 25219 took us along a sadly neglected line (now called the Tarka Line in a feeble attempt to attract more passengers). For me, perversely, the dereliction was all part of its charm. A summer shower had wet the old stations and they smelled of rust and rotten wood. Two decades before, when these stations were full of life, children from Bristol and London would have been looking through the windows, impatient for the woods to thin, and for the skies to expand in the way they do when the sea lies sparkling beyond the next hill.

I boasted to people that my railway trips made me into an observer and chronicler of life, that alongside all the numbers in my notebooks I made witty observations of British culture. But, re-reading, I've realized that so much of it is trivia and absolute rubbish. 'Barnstaple – scruffy brown dog chasing carrier-bag. Plymouth – had a cup of tea. Exeter – man asleep on seat. Newquay – cup of tea and digestive biscuit. Cardiff – Bounty and orange Fanta.' There are annotated snatches of conversation too:

Cockney lad: 'They've got to move the train because it's too long for the platform.'
Posh woman with hairdo: 'If I can't get a sleeper I shall go in the first class.'

And the odd thing is that I can remember all these people quite clearly.

Further down the line, after a trip down the Gunnislake branch, we paused for dinner. Despite the self-incriminating evidence in my notebooks, a trainspotter's life isn't all crisps and Kit-Kats and British Rail tea. We were capable of modest attempts at self-catering. A small sliced Hovis and a pack of cheese slices will provide a spotter with a whole pile of sandwiches as easily as shuffling a deck of cards. But I'd long ago learned not to bother with a flask. You set off with good intentions and a satisfying pint of cream of chicken soup, but it needed such self-discipline, washing it out thoroughly, asking for a refill at a café or station buffet, swilling it out again. I'd never got past the first step and always ended up carrying the empty flask around all week. Well, not quite empty. Tightly sealed, stewing up its warm bacteria-rich fumes, that remaining spoonful of chicken soup could turn itself into a salmonella time-bomb. A week later, when the flask was opened, the mould sprang out like a magician's bouquet.

In some ways this trip was a reprise of the one we didn't make in 1968. It wasn't the last steamers we were chasing this time, but the last Westerns (I only needed six more for the set). Yet, steam or diesel, the urgency was the same. The chase was the thing; the mission to record something endangered before it had gone for good. This time, though, we could be more involved. We were old enough to appreciate the occasion, and solvent enough to afford all the chasing up and down between Penzance and Paddington. Yet for all that, we were totally powerless. Nothing we could say or do could halt the march of progress; 1968 came and went, as would 1975.

The ferry trip across the River Exe at Starcross was one I'd always wanted to make. I don't know why. I think I just liked the name. Starcross had a kind of mythical sound to it, the kind of place elves lived. Jinx wasn't that keen (he never liked wasting good spotting time), but I wheedled my way. We sat in the sunshine to wait for the ferry while the holiday trains clattered alongside the mudflats, a blur of happy pink faces and summer colours moving above our heads.

One reservation I had was that Jinx and I were so unanimous about our affection for Warships and Westerns that there was no dissent, no argument. It made for a quiet life, and, if I was totally honest, I missed the East-West rivalry and all the bitchery about each other's love lives that I'd shared with Andy Parker.

Jinx had been married for three years already, but his wife was tolerant of his trainspotting urge. Since it wasn't costing him any money, she could hardly attack him with the standard (and justified) complaint of many wives: that he was squandering money better spent on groceries and household improvements. All in all he had it cushy, and without the underlying current of dissatisfaction, our friendship lacked a dramatic edge. We were just two trainspotters out on a jaunt.

There was another thing I wasn't so happy about. Unnoticed by me, British Rail had changed all its loco numbers. The new system was called TOPS and was supposed to make life easier for everyone. Some of it was logical: Deltic 9001 became 55001 and 8100 became 20100. But much of it seemed random and baffling to me: 9000 became 55022 (because the primitive computers of the time couldn't recognize 55000), 1783 became 47301 and 5536 became 31118. It made me feel very uneasy. How could I be sure that it was all bona fide, that the re-numbering hadn't been massaged or cocked-up? I might be chasing numbers, unaware that I'd really seen them before, thinking an engine was a cop when it wasn't. It seemed dangerous to me, like meddling with the holy code, force-feeding the digits of the computer age into the ramshackle homeliness of the railways. 9001 I could like, 55001 I just couldn't get used to.

Still, they hadn't bothered re-numbering the Westerns

because they weren't going to be around long enough to take part in the computer-age railway.

Regional railrovers like this Western one, while limited in scope, had a lot of advantages. With a smaller area to cover, there was time to take it easy and look properly at things. Unlike the All-Line Railrover I'd been on with Andy, you didn't feel you had to see every inch of Britain in seven days and make yourself sick doing it. I'd been to many of these Western places before, but we broke some new ground, like the three branch lines to Fishguard, Pembroke and Milford Haven in Wales. There were few locos to be seen this far west, apart from the occasional shunter and a Brush with a trainload of oil tanks. But that didn't bother us, as it wasn't locos we were after, merely the status of having done these remote lines.

Despite having a sleeper service to Paddington, Milford Haven turned out to be little more than a halt, with no comforts at all. Even the single luggage trolley was chained up and looked as if it hadn't been used for ten years. Yet I liked these forgotten corners and took a perverse pleasure in the kind of neglect I really ought to have been protesting about.

A couple of sedative pints in the pub across the road set us up for a pleasant overnight kip to Paddington. Everything seemed perfect – we were alone in one of three old coaches rattling through the Welsh night – until we arrived at Swansea, and three hundred people off the Cork ferry tried to cram in alongside us. One of the worst things about overnight travel is that awful moment when you're woken from a pleasant doze by a load of strangers and – smiling, of course, in that English way – you know that now you've got to sit up all the way to your destination. Even if you do get any sleep it'll be with your head lolling, swinging around like Linda Blair in *The Exorcist*, before you wake up with a jolt, dribbling, and everyone else slyly enjoying your embarrassment.

Why was I still pretending this was a 'holiday' when so many of my old schoolmates were jetting off and spending two calm weeks in Greece or Spain? How could I argue that tea and crisps in the Swindon buffet was in any way comparable to cocktails by the pool and girls in swimsuits? Two nights later, despairing of finding a seat on the overnight to Paddington, we baled out at Exeter St Davids and bedded down in a small waiting room on Platform 2. The place was about as big as a garden shed. But no one disturbed us and we managed to get some sleep on the hard wooden benches, before catching a Paddington train the next morning. My back was killing me. Even at the tender age of twenty-two I was already thinking that these nocturnal adventures were too much for me. Still, unlike my ill-fated railrover with Andy, at least Jinx and I had managed to see this one through to its conclusion.

I haven't been on a railrover since 1975, not in Britain. These trips of 1973 and 1975 would be impossible to repeat – not least because there are scarcely any overnight trains left. There are posh sleepers to and from Scotland, and one to Cornwall, but no meandering unhurried trains, which is just one more part of railway life that's changed out of all recognition to us old-time bashers. Twenty years ago the railways still had a nightlife. Insomniacs and wide-awake children who lived by the railway could still sit by their windows and see the yellow lights of the compartments and the dark shapes of heads. Spotters could still find plenty to occupy them at places like Bristol, Leeds or Manchester, and there were plenty of trains they could doss down on. It wasn't just the major routes, there were all kinds of eccentric overnight workings, mail and parcels trains with a couple of carriages tacked on behind just in case. As recently as 1980 you could travel overnight from York to Aberystwyth, via Huddersfield and Manchester, arriving at 7 a.m.; or go in the opposite direction on the night service from Manchester to Cleethorpes, arriving at the awful washed-out hour of 5 a.m.

The overnight trains have gone, and with them much of the railways' mystery and sense of adventure. Yes, waiting for them was often cold and uncomfortable, but there was a definite magic to those midnight stations: the deserted platforms, the ticking clock with its burping springs, the sudden rush of a 3-tank milk train, the red and green signal lights, the boxes of flowers to be delivered to London by dawn, the mailbags dragged along the platform like murder victims to be disposed of . . .

Lying flat out on the dusty seats, drugged by the lingering odours from decades of mackintoshes and twin-sets, there was something comforting and nostalgic in those leftover smells from years gone by. The old sound of wheels on a railway track still has much in common with the ticking of clocks or the sound of steady rain; it slips in with the rhythms of the body, a syncopated slow-burning jazz session that lulls you to sleep.

014   King's Cross Solitaire

In 1975 I got a lowly clerical job in the Department of Trade and went off to live in London. One Saturday in September my mum stood at the window and watched me go, dressed in my new blue suit, dragging my suitcase to the station for what must have been the saddest train journey of my life. She'd seen me off for the station many times in the past ten years, but this time I didn't have a flask of soup, and nor would I be home at teatime with a bookful of numbers to sort out.

Newly installed in a hostel for young civil servants in Highbury I felt lost and homesick. Everyone else seemed to be pals already, and I was too shy to speak up and join in. The social options were on the stark side: snooker, ping-pong, a smoke-filled TV room, or getting rat-arsed in the Hen and Chickens, none of which remotely appealed.

Alone, one always looks for one's security blanket, and so, naturally, I turned to the trains. Every evening, after a hostel dinner of chicken supreme or mince stew, I left the others to their chess games and pub crawls and took the Victoria Line down to King's Cross. Standing at the end of Platform 8 with a fag and a notebook I felt happy and at home. The Deltics were still in charge of the Scottish expresses, and reminded me of the thrill and the hint of fear as they'd roared through Grantham. And that was part of the reason I found King's Cross such a comfort. It connected me to home, not just physically – I could always jump on a train and escape – but spiritually too. Alone in a city of eight million people, just another solitary figure on a London station, I could still reach out and run my fingers across the green paintwork of the same Deltic that had thrilled me as a kid.

But I wasn't totally alone. In common with most hobbies, trainspotting has an underlying social function, offering all kinds of people a ready-made excuse to talk to each other. I wasn't a chatterbox, I kept myself to myself, but I wouldn't ignore anyone if they talked to me. There was always someone who wanted to know what loco had been on the 7.30 Leeds–Harrogate, or whether any Scottish Brush had been sighted, and I was happy to provide the answers. But I resisted any further plays for friendship – even a simple drink in the buffet could lead to all kinds of complications. I could tell that some of these people were lonely, but while I rather enjoyed my solitude, these men in belted raincoats were too obviously sad and lonely, and possibly slightly mad.

I remember one who scared me, a quietly spoken middle-aged man whose breath smelt of TCP. He'd latched on to me, persisting with all kinds of not-quite-right questions: 'Has the 14.29 gone yet?' (It was past seven at night) and 'Is Jack booked for the Aberdeen sleeper?' (Who the hell was Jack anyway?). I was getting bored and fidgety, wishing him away, scared to move myself in case he followed me. I was just plucking up the courage to be rude to him, when I happened to glance at his *Combine*. The pages were totally unmarked, except for three diesel shunters I knew quite well were based in Swansea. Immediately alarmed, I understood then that I was in the presence of somebody quite deranged. I made my excuses and left, constantly turning to check if he was following me. He was, and I had to dash down into the Underground to lose myself in the crowds. Ten minutes later I went back, but to another platform. But I was forever on the look-out after that and never felt quite as relaxed as I had.

From the suburban platforms on the west side of the station, I watched the last commuters of the day heading back to the dormitory towns of Hertfordshire. I no longer bothered with the feverish task of taking bog unit numbers, but I was fascinated by this twilight exodus from the city. And jealous. Bathed in the yellow light of their carriages, they were all going home to their neat suburban houses, their pretty wives and cuddlesome children. It made me awfully homesick and I began to dread the boredom and routine of the hostel. My inner feelings can be guessed from this snippet of an unfinished novel which I recently found scribbled in the back of my spotting book:

> Mark sat in the buffet at King's Cross station with
> a pint of bitter and a half-full pack of cigarettes. A
> cartridge player was churning out pop music.
> Mark spent many of his evenings at King's Cross,
> primarily to watch the trains, a joy since
> childhood, but also because it was a comforting
> haven, an easy reference point in London, a city
> of 8 million assorted egos.

An enduring fascination with stations helped keep me loyal to the railways when I eventually stopped collecting train numbers a couple of years after this King's Cross period. However indifferent people have become to trains, anyone with a smidgin of poetry in their soul can't fail to be fascinated by the comings and goings of a railway station. Or am I just dealing in clichés? I know that for me, all the years I'd been a trainspotter, I'd always felt I saw something my mates didn't. The railways had a transport function, of course, but they had a poetic function too, a cultural overlay that no PR department have ever understood and one that no politicians will ever succeed in privatizing.

After the 20.00 had departed for Aberdeen (the same train Andy and I had been on two years previously), I made my way back to the hostel, stopping off for egg fried rice from the Chinkie (as it was widely called then). Back at the hostel I sat on my bed and gobbled it up with the plastic fork. Since you weren't supposed to bring food in, I had the choice of opening the window and freezing or risking discovery because of the Oriental aromas seeping out of the room. The hurry and the worry always spoiled the enjoyment.

Dutiful son that I was, I rang my mum every other night. But I didn't tell her about my evenings at King's Cross because there'd recently been a TV programme about runaways and the seedy sexual nightlife centred around the station. I'd never seen anything untoward, but to avoid worrying my mum unduly, I told her I went to Paddington, as if that was somehow more respectable. Being whisked away by a gay press gang didn't worry me, but I was scared of being blown to bits by the IRA. The mid-seventies were a nervy time, and when there weren't real bombs there were dozens of false alarms. At least one night a week my trainspotting was interrupted by an order to evacuate the station. It upset me to think that my safe world of railways was threatened by dark cruel forces. I could be safely jotting down numbers one moment and simply ceasing to exist the next.

Everyone had a dose of the jitters, and when I went to the Deltics' home depot at Finsbury Park one evening I got very short shrift from the Cockney foreman.

'How do I know you're a bloody trainspotter? You could be a bloody IRA terrorist for all I know.'

He was right, of course, and couldn't be blamed for being vigilant – though I refrained from pointing out that he'd hardly be ticking me off like a kid if I was a real terrorist. After years of carefree trespass on British Rail property it came as a shock to realize that it could be liable to misinterpretation. I felt it was a slur too – as if I'd ever do anything except simply walk round and jot down numbers. Couldn't they see I was just an off-duty civil servant, a simple trainspotter, as loyal to the nation as they were? In retrospect I suppose I should count myself lucky not to have been jumped on by the Special Branch and given a good kicking.

A few years later, in the spring of 1978, I finally got myself a job with British Rail. It was only a humble clerical post in the Traveller's Fare offices at King's Cross, but it meant precious travel concessions. Like Jinx, I'd soon be able to travel to Inverness for a couple of quid or shoot off to Poland to get a last whiff of steam. That was the theory, but it turned out to be just another crummy job in a long line of crummy jobs.

This vital part of BR's catering operation was housed in a crumbling slum at the back of King's Cross station, in a street now notorious for its prostitutes and inner city decay. What had once been a bustling railway quarter full of parcels offices and railwaymen's houses had become a windswept rat-run. Grass grew on the pavement, and the downstairs door of our offices bore the bootprints of down-and-outs who'd tried to break in for a kip in the hallway.

The job entailed looking at all the dockets from the dining cars and checking them off against the cheques and credit card slips. Besides me there were two other clerks. A moody girl from Newcastle called Moira, and Myra, an old biddy who wore cardigans and had a stick through her greying bun. The similarity in names didn't help much. Every time I called one, I always got the other. It led to a lot of irritation on all sides.

Our boss was an Indian, a gentlemanly type from Bombay who proudly considered himself Anglicized. But I couldn't understand a word he said. He'd had to go through the job routine twice with me, but at the end I was none the wiser, and I never did quite twig it. The offices were laughably Dickensian, a century away from the gas-powered chairs and ergonomic desks of the modern scene. Some of the ink blots had been there for a century, and I couldn't help but be fascinated by the ownerless trilby on the hat stand. Myra said it had belonged to a previous employee who had jumped under a Tube train in 1971 and they were all too superstitious to touch it.

Bored silly and prone to daydreams that Billy Liar would find embarrassing, even a luncheon bill could set my imagination off. I made up little conversations in my head, and whole scripts for murder mysteries which I would type up in the evening and send off to the BBC the following day.

BILL: I'll get this, Fred. (He gets up from the table.) Must visit the little boy's room.

FRED: If this Vienna deal's going to go through, Tom, we'd better make sure McGinty doesn't talk.

TOM: He won't, Fred. I'll make sure of that.

I don't know whether my mouth moved as I made up these *Murder on the 5.10* screenplays, but Moira gave me some very strange looks during the day. Moira looked at me a lot, if the truth were told, sometimes in a mooning sort of way, which I thought might be lovesickness, but at other times it looked more like pure contempt. I couldn't make it out. But being young and male I couldn't fail to notice her female charms. Unlike Myra, swathed in old cardigans smelling of Mothax, Moira had the desk nearest to the electric fire and wore white blouses thin enough to show her lacy bra. All in all we seemed to spend a lot of time looking at each other, then looking away when caught out. In the end, I decided she did fancy me and resolved to take a chance.

One evening I caught her at the bus stop after work. She was glad of my company, as a couple of days previously she'd been kerb-crawled by a creep in a Cortina. She'd been seething about it all week: couldn't a girl wear nice clothes without some awful man getting the wrong idea? I made sympathetic noises and tried to crank my bravado into action before her bus came lumbering along. Moira was one of those people who always seemed to live in the most obscure parts of London – Palmers Green, Walthamstow or Hammersmith. They thought they lived in London, but they could never let their hair down, they were always too worried about getting home to have any fun. If I'd had a car I'd have been halfway there with her. As it was I had only my wits to rely on.

'We could nip in the pub for a drink,' I suggested, knowing quite well we'd have a stiff walk before we found a decent pub in that area.

'I've got to get back. I've got to wash my hair. And *Coronation Street*'s on tonight.'

'You don't need to wash it. It looks lovely as it is.'

Moira looked at me pityingly, curled a finger round a lock of hair and let it go as if in disgust. 'It's awful.'

A friend had once told me that compliments always worked, but he hadn't given me Plan B, what to do when the compliments were rejected out of hand. Moira's disappointment was tangible.

'You could always come back to Belsize Park,' I said. 'Not so far to travel in the morning, then.'

It was said in a jokey sort of way, but the suggestion that intimacy could be taken for granted obviously disgusted her. Spoiled by the easy morality that prevailed in Belsize Park, I mistakenly assumed that everyone was dying for it. Moira may have been making sheep's eyes at me, she may not. But I'd blown it completely: she was a girl who wanted flowers and candlelit meals, not a bedsit one-nighter in NW3.

I dreaded going in the next day. From the dirty looks I got as soon as I walked in, Moira had obviously told Myra every sordid detail. The kerb-crawler had been knocked from No.1 spot in the creep's gallery by a sex-mad clerk. The atmosphere was awful. I kept expecting Myra to whip the stick out of her hair and stab me, but she contented herself with ignoring me when tea was made. Unable to face their silent reproof and the sheer boredom of the job, I jacked it in and went back on the dole. If I'd had a hat I might have left it behind as a memento, but I have a feeling that Moira would have taken it off the peg and chucked it in the bin.

015 Trans Europ Express: Paris, 1975

If you set any store by poets or brochures, November is hardly the best time of year for your first-ever visit to Paris. But when I had a surprise tax rebate in my wages one Friday, I knew it was time to go. There was no planning. I just walked round to Liverpool Street station during my lunch-hour and slapped down a sheaf of fivers in exchange for a big white ticket to Europe. Eight hours later I was at Victoria, standing in the queue for the overnight ferry service via Dunkirk. While my fellow passengers had rucksacks patched with sew-on badges, or suitcases with squeaky wheels, my only luggage was an Argos carrier bag with an *Evening Standard*, a Topic and a packet of Embassy. If I looked eccentric, I was happily unaware of it.

It was the first time I'd been to Victoria, and until then I'd always imagined it as important and impressive. In fact it was dreary and suburban. Like many people,

I'd romanticized foreign travel and, as a trainspotter, added on the idea of going by *The Golden Arrow*, one of those great British trains that had worked its way into young minds, exerting a subliminal patriotism. But back then, before the Eurostars, trains to Dover were the same bog units as commuters used, with three or four of them coupled together, rarely swept out, sometimes unheated, and no refreshments. Still, if there were banana skins in the ashtray and scrumpled newspapers on the seats, I didn't care. The adventure blinded me to the grubbiness of the train and the dreary suburbs which seemed to stretch out all the way to the coast.

It occurred to me on the ferry that my mum had no idea where I was, and she'd have had a fit if she'd seen me. In my haste to get to France I hadn't given a thought to appropriate dress and had only had a skinny maroon jacket to protect me from the freezing mists. 'Daft as a brush,' she'd have said. I couldn't expect Mum to understand, but in those days, when I still smoked, the glow of a fag-end was enough to keep me warm. This was exactly how it should be: leaning on the deck-rail as a lighthouse beam swept the black and glassy water, watching the smudge of French coastline get nearer and clearer, its mists slipping aside like torn curtains to reveal the overgrown Meccano cranes of Dunkirk docks.

Off the ferry and through French customs, I scurried down the echoing corridors to the station, eager for my first taste of French railways. What a shock. Dappled by greasy shadows from the docks, the waiting train was green and gloomy and about fifty years old. No *Flèche d'Or* this end either. Even so, as I walked along the low platforms to have a look at what engine would be pulling us, the carriages with their 'Dunkerque–Lille–Arras–Paris' signboards towered above me, importantly and mysteriously. I muttered those foreign names to myself, like a kind of spell or incantation, nervous of the magic they might unleash. That was the attraction of travel –

the danger, the novelty, which had nothing to do with whether the train was new or clean.

I found myself a compartment and sat there shivering, with no idea what time the train might depart. Leaning down, I felt a faint breath from the heater under the seat, but it was hardly enough to make life cosy. Still, I was a trainspotter, such rigours were par for the course. What did I expect, a Pullman chair and a brass light to read the *FT* by? The important thing was that with the same old touchstones – sliding door, luggage rack, squeaking seat arms – I felt perfectly safe, in my natural habitat. Stretching myself out on the slippery brown seat, I slipped into unconsciousness and dozed my way to Paris.

I'd never seen French people *en masse* before, so it was a shock when the train jerked to a halt at a suburban station (St Denis, I think), and I woke to see a platform full of miserable workers staring back at me. Wiping the dozy dribble from the side of my mouth, I ducked down out of their sight until the train moved on.

Sleep might have claimed me again, but tired and stiff as I was, I couldn't miss leaning out of the window for my first views of Paris. Suburbs of cities had always fascinated me, the way houses and shops and factories gradually start sticking alongside the railway, accumulating and jostling for space, spreading backwards until, suddenly, there's a full-blown metropolis, honking and smoggy and coloured with giant posters.

Minutes later I stepped from the train. Walking down the platform at the Gare du Nord I felt full of it, like Sinatra in some MGM musical. 'My kinda town, Paris is . . .' My Argos carrier bag didn't matter here, in fact it must have looked foreign and chic. I skipped down the steps to the Metro and made straight for the map of lines, quickly sussing out how the system worked and which line I wanted. I stood close to the ticket window and watched what everyone else did, how much they paid, then I just walked up and followed suit. It worked a treat. This is all part of trainspotting pride, this rapid assimilation of knowledge and quickness to pick up a routine.

But it's easy to get caught out. When the train drew in I waited like a lemon for the doors to hiss open as they do in London. I waited and waited, until the Parisians behind me exploded with impatience and pushed past to flick the handle.

I loved the Metro immediately. The trains were blue and cream with rubber tyres, so clean and quietly efficient after London's Northern Line. It wasn't just the trains, but the whole ambiance: the bready smell, the warning hooters, the sad Africans with their lazy brooms. But what charmed me most of all were the posters. Instead of far-fetched promises like 'Your company will love moving to Peterborough' there were naked women luxuriating in perfumed soap lather. You couldn't smell the lather, and yet you knew it was gorgeous. Even the housewives advertising frozen peas were chic and sexy. The Paris Metro was an erotic wonderland.

With so much travelling behind me, I thought of myself as worldly-wise, but it was laughable arrogance, and I was soon caught on the hop yet again. So sure that the rue Montmartre Metro station was Montmartre, it came as a disappointment, and a blow to my pride, when I surfaced in an anonymous-looking street I knew damn well wasn't the famous bohemian quarter. Still, I was quite happy to wander at random. I tried out my French on an old woman in a tobacco kiosk, but all I got from her was a baffled glare, and to get a pack of Marlboro I had to resort to pointing like a child.

I hadn't gone to Paris with the intention of trainspotting (would anyone be such a dullard?), and I started off with the best intentions – walking the scrunchy paths of the Tuileries, clocking the Eiffel Tower, pacing the squeaking floors of the Musée d'Art Moderne – but some homing instinct guided my feet towards the Gare de Lyon.

We all collude in the pretence that purée de pommes de terre is somehow tastier than mashed potatoes, but why should the Gare de Lyon be any more interesting than King's Cross or Paddington? Why romanticize everything on the strength of a foreign name? But the Gare de Lyon *was* different; here was one of the nodal points of Europe and every clattering of the indicator boards signalled the chance of adventure. *Le Mistral*, *Le Capitole*, *Puerto del Sol*, and what was left of the Orient Express – this was the place where all those grand expresses departed from. You could board a train here and alight in a land of fezes and minarets. Even the commuter trains were different – instead of Traceys and Sharons gum-chewing their way through the *Sun* the sodium-grey units were full of stylish and bright-eyed girls reading Gallimard paperbacks.

I wasn't writing down any engine numbers (they would have been meaningless to me) but I couldn't resist wandering to the end of the platform to take some souvenir snaps of the silver and orange electric trains which, with their angled front ends, looked like sprinters poised at the block, ready for the pistol and the graceful dash down to Dijon. The drivers looked at me suspiciously and, though I didn't think the French were as paranoid about trainspotters as the Soviets, I decided not to push my luck. After my feeble attempt to buy Marlboro, how on earth would I explain the trainspotting bug to a bunch of cynical French policemen?

The Gare de Lyon wasn't the only place that snared me. I was heavily into Sartre's *The Age of Reason* just then, the opening sentence of which begins: 'Halfway down the Rue Vercingétorix . . .', and, just like any daft tourist, I wanted to go and stand there for myself. But forty years had passed since Sartre had written his book and the street was half-derelict now, full of empty houses and boarded-up shops, a real let-down. There was no point in asking anyone to take a souvenir shot of me; the few people I saw hanging around looked more likely to run off with my camera and pawn it for the price of a bottle of Rémy Martin.

Still, didn't it also say, 'A railway engine whistled, and Mathieu thought: "I'm getting old"'? If that was true, there had to be railways close by – the line from the Gare Montparnasse. I turned a corner and found myself on a bridge overlooking a goods depot where a sage green BB loco shunted wagons up and down. The Gare de Lyon may have been exciting, but it was big and public, lacking in privacy. This, however, was the kind of spot I could have made my own, a kind of Parisian Wetmore Sidings.

After a few minutes I came to my senses. Was I crazy? I hadn't come to Paris to go trainspotting. Worse, I was probably a trespasser. I could end up in the 14th arrondissement clink at this rate. Trainspotting was stuck in my head, I couldn't just leave my interest behind at Dover.

I quickly got back on the tourist trail (Notre Dame, the Louvre) but by teatime I was back at the Gare du Nord, with time for a station hot dog and a beer before finding a seat on the train back to Dunkirk. I'd managed to get myself coffee and croissants in a café, but felt too timid to try booking into a hotel or sitting in a restaurant for a proper meal. But even if it had been little more than a day trip, I'd broken the hold of Britain, and was the first of our old gang to do so. From then on the whole of Europe lay at my feet. I would be Trans Europ Express Man, whizzing from København to München (it had to be the proper spellings now), smoking international brands and humming Abba's greatest hits.

016 Commuting: Just a Way of Getting From A to B

I've been lucky to escape the soul-destroying nine-to-five routine of the commuter, but in the mid-seventies I was travelling by train so often that, for a while, the railways were in danger of losing their charm. Every Friday I caught the 16.10 from Euston – same platform, same carriages, same faces – to spend the weekend in Burton. I didn't mind this sameness so much on Fridays; I was homeward bound, after all, with lots to tell my friends and, after a week of hostel dinners and Chinese take-aways, a feast of Mum's home cooking to get stuck into. It was the Monday mornings I hated, fighting for a seat on the 7.18 from New Street with a load of Brummie businessmen. They thought they were early birds, but to me they looked more like Christmas turkeys. I could laugh at them, but my laughter had a nervous edge to it.

What I disliked most was not the routine so much as the crowds. We don't like each other much *en masse*, if the truth's told. Ideally we'd all like four seats and a table to ourselves, the space and privacy to take off our shoes, bite our nails, give up on the crossword without feeling publicly stupid. Nostalgia merchants go on about the Golden Age of rail travel: sharing compartments, talking to each other, enduring delays and cock-ups with real Blitz spirit. There may be a small element of truth in it, but it's mostly legend. If the truth were known, it was just a stiff upper lip show. We hated the smell of each other's lives, really. What we were yearning for all that time was the freedom of the car age: the freedom to pick our noses, to flash the V-sign at people and make a quick escape, to sing tunelessly along with 'Strangers in the Night' on the radio. We make all these sad noises about steam trains, bus conductresses and corner shops, but we couldn't wait to get rid of them all.

Just as I was finishing the book and wondering if this was, on reflection, too harsh, a Tory transport minister endorsed it with his support for cars. 'You have your own company, your own temperature control, your own music – and you don't have to put up with dreadful human beings sitting alongside you.' The problem here, of course, is that we can't all afford to travel by car – it would be havoc if we all did so – and conditions are so bad on public transport precisely because road-building has taken precedence over investment in public transport during the last fifteen years.

These businessmen had no time for chatting anyway, they were too preoccupied with finding ways to look important. Mobile phones and lap-tops are the currency now, but things used to be more modest. The snap of locks on a briefcase, the click of a Parker biro, some ticks and scribbles on a document, such simple gestures were enough to mark you as a vital cog in British commerce. (I always wondered just what all these papers were. Top-secret M.O.D. files are always turning up in skips or being left on the Tube, but those businessmen never left any evidence behind. Perhaps it was for the best. I'd have been quite disappointed to find out those documents were nothing more than paperclip sales by region or the marketing strategy for a new vacuum cleaner bag.)

Faced with all this importance (though I could never take Brummie businessmen completely seriously) I felt self-conscious about trainspotting. I no longer had a valid excuse. I wasn't a kid any more, beardless and eager and safely ignored. Whenever I looked up from jotting down a number or two on the edge of my newspaper, people smirked and looked away. Or perhaps it was just my paranoia. Was it a smirk that guy let slip? Or might it have been a smile, a secret signal that, despite the shirt and tie, he was part of the brotherhood? I didn't dare take the risk. To start talking to strangers about trains would have immediately marked me as a kind of nutter. And so I began to let things go, over-powered by public opinion. If I had had the carriage to myself I'd have enjoyed it. Instead I pretended I was just another commuter with nothing better to do than read the paper.

To be honest, there wasn't that much to see anyway. I still needed a few of the electric locos on the West Coast main line, but apart from what I glimpsed at Coventry or Rugby, it all flashed past so quickly – a thump of squashed air against the window and a blur of blue and white livery – there was no hope of getting any numbers. Someone had shifted the gears and moved trainspotting into the fast lane. But this speed wasn't there to thrill trainspotters, its purpose was to blur, to marginalize everything between A and B. These trains had windows, but you weren't really supposed to be that interested in the outside world, businessmen supposedly had better things to do than look at sheep and canal boats.

Things were improving on the railways. But they were much less interesting. The new Mk II carriages were comfy and warm, double-glazed and brightly up-holstered, yet as sterile as a DHSS waiting room. I felt sorry for the men who were trying to catch forty winks in these seats, which had never been designed for dozers. But this was the future: democratic, open-plan, purpose-designed. All the trains were identical now and even the passengers were beginning to look suspiciously alike.

I missed the past: the seats smelling of pre-war dust and the luggage racks made of knotted string. I wanted those nose-height windows you could snap open for a reviving gust of wind and the long seats ideal for sprawl-ing out on.

Why was I being so churlish? Wasn't it wonderful to have an illuminated 'Vacant' sign to eliminate pointless journeys to the toilet? But did we really want everyone in the carriage to know we were going for a wee? All the new technology couldn't stop men losing their aim whenever the train swayed and returning to their seats sideways so you couldn't see the splash on their trousers.

Still, wasn't this what we'd all, railway management and trainspotters alike, dreamed about: the train of the future, wired up with shaving-points and a PA system to keep the travelling public up-to-date? 'This is Rugby. This is Rugby . . .' It was as if travellers had suddenly gone blind. Did they really think we couldn't see the rather large station just outside the window? British Rail was smooth-talking us into believing in a new railway age, but it seemed to necessitate treating us all like babies.

I always perked up as we passed the loco depot at Willesden in London, and I'd even allow myself a muttered 'yes!' if I copped anything. The suits were too busy to take any notice of me by then, they were all getting ready for the race, locking briefcases, folding newspapers, edging away down the train. Some made for the nearest door, happy to be first out of their carriage. But a few had to make their way right down the train to the very end door. Window down, hand on handle, tense and ready to twist, each one hoped to be the very first person to step off the train at Euston. Sad little triumphs. But it was frighteningly easy to become just like them. I could see myself all too clearly, just another shop dummy standing on the escalator as it went deep deep deep into the ground to deliver me to my job in the City. Was this it then, the end of adventure? Train travel was no longer a lark, it was just a way of getting from one soulless station to another.

This was all in 1976, but it's not so very different now. Only the faces have changed, and the sad thing is that not all of them have; many of them have been shuttling up and down this line for the past twenty years.

One day there was a guy on the train with a radio-cassette. They were as big as suitcases in those days, but he'd wired it up so he could listen to his music through

A northbound express heads into the mouth of the tunnel
at Primrose Hill in London

those spongiform ear-cooking headphones. The suits
from Tipton and Walsall stared at him as if he was a
freak. But not me, I stared with admiration. This man
(he had an anorak and a small beard) was a herald of
the future. If only they could miniaturize that, I thought,
they'd be on to a real winner. Everyone will want to do
it. Even the suits from Tipton and Walsall had James
Last tapes they'd rather listen to than read the *Telegraph*.
And sure enough, five years later the Sony Walkman
arrived. I've conjured up reams of philosophy on my
travels, but that was the only time I'd predicted the
future.

017   Strangers on a Train: The China Clay Special

I hadn't seen Jinx for about a year, so I was surprised when he got in touch to ask if I wanted to go on a trip with him. The China Clay Special was a spotters' bash, a 12-coach train ('408 tons approx' boasted the brochure) hauled from London to Cornwall by one of the last remaining Westerns ('5400 h.p. gross' we were reminded).

These details didn't interest me, but they were obviously important to some people. Trainspotting involves a lot of punter's maths. Here, for instance, how well could a 5400 h.p. Western cope with a 12-coach 408-ton train? What would be the optimum speed? And how would that be affected by gradients, signal slows or wet rails? There were a lot of parallels with horse-racing, and like racing a spotters' bash has its poetic edge. Just as racegoers get aroused by the panting horses, the shining sweat and the thud of iron on turf, so trainspotters get a similar thrill from the growling, throbbing, kicking effort of a Western, Whistler or Hoover.

What did interest me was a day at the seaside. After its roundabout trip via Bristol, Plymouth and Falmouth the train would end up in Newquay with the promise of a pint and a fish and chip lunch. It sounded like it might be fun, and after a year in London I needed a refreshing blast of ozone, so I told Jinx to get me a ticket.

He was flabbergasted when I turned up to meet him at Paddington. Instead of the regulation rucksack with dangling laces, I had a bulging suitcase with me. I'd jacked in my job, flitted from the hostel and was on my way home, via Newquay. The China Clay was as good a way as any and, on the return trip, I could change at Bristol for a train to Burton.

I'd been happy with my job at Companies House, but they'd just transferred me to Millbank Tower, a horrid glassy monolith on the banks of the Thames. I hated it. My new office was so high up that the morning mist didn't clear till midday. When it did I could see the trains going in and out of Waterloo, but it brought me no pleasure; they were so far below I felt like I was looking at the world through the wrong end of binoculars. All in all, things were no better than any of those awful factories I'd worked in, so it was inevitable that I'd stick two fingers up to it before a month was out.

Despite one or two curious looks, no one wanted to know why I had such formal luggage with me. If I looked a bit glum, no one remarked on it or tried to cheer me up. They were too excited by the prospect of the trip and I should have known better than to bring along a parcel of emotional problems to embarrass everyone with. I stowed the suitcase up on the luggage rack and tried to forget it was there.

As we passed Old Oak Common sheds around midnight, everyone rushed to the windows for a glimpse of 50s and 31s parked under the floodlights. This was what they all wanted to be part of, this 24-hours-a-day man's world, walking down the lines with their lamps swinging, loosening couplings and connecting air-brakes. But I couldn't join in this collective envy of railwaymen. Nor was I in the mood for sticking my head out into a rushing slipstream. I'd become more self-conscious during my time in London, and bothered more about my appearance. I didn't want to arrive in Cornwall looking like Worzel Gummidge.

Trainspotters' specials are still immensely popular. Their names get wackier each year: The Tatty Cat, The Whistle Test, The Hymn 'n' Ham, The Welsh Rarebit. And they come in all shapes and sizes: non-stop runs

1068 *Western Reliance* leaving Paddington with a Cardiff train in 1973

from Paddington to Penzance; loco endurance tests on the Settle–Carlisle line ('Listen to that beast!'); or specially routed excursions which squeeze along freight lines no normal passenger ever sees. These trips have been going for decades, pre-dating trainspotting itself. They're from the era when an interest in railways was a suitable pursuit for educated gentlemen, and this history is reflected in august names like the Stephenson Locomotive Society and the Railway Correspondence and Travel Society.

The China Clay reached Bristol at 02.35. I was just beginning to doze off by then, but Jinx and the others were in no mood to waste a trip dozing. We had an hour's wait, plenty of time to fetch tea and Kit-Kats from the buffet, set up cameras to take time-exposures of 31s on newspaper trains, or just sit nattering. Trainspotters are a scattered tribe, but they all get to know each other sooner or later. Most of the people on the train were Western Region nuts and they'd shared tea and train stories at Taunton and Plymouth and Swindon. As more and more spotters chased fewer and fewer Westerns, they'd all ended up in the same places at the same time. The China Clay wasn't just any old trip, it was a club outing and an old boys' reunion rolled into one.

Unlike so many of these spotters, I'd never been interested in the mechanics of trains. Exactly what a diesel-hydraulic was, I'd never had the foggiest, nor any inclination to find out. I didn't know what a torque converter was (the Western had six) nor did I give a toss whether the driving wheels were 3ft 7in as against the Warship's 3ft 3½in. I suppose it made some difference, but I just didn't care. I liked Westerns because they were maroon. But I knew that wasn't quite what I was expected to say. Imagine their faces if I'd chipped in with some airy-fairy nonsense about maroon livery touched by the light of a Bristol dawn, or the ragged cloud of diesel floating above the bright-faced holidaymakers at Dawlish.

I couldn't understand these men liking the Westerns for the sole reason that they were diesel-hydraulic, and nor could I understand why, as a result, they despised diesel-electrics. But it actually mattered to them and they could keep up fervent conversations with each other about the most obscure details:

HANK: The Warship's MD650 does more revs than the 655. It was technically a better engine.

NEV: Yes, but it's thrashing the shit out of itself. You're talking about twice as much time in maintenance.

HANK: They should never have transferred the Warships to the Waterloo–Exeter in the first place.

NEV: Yeah, all that starting and stopping really put the mockers on them.

I had neither the knowledge nor the desire to join in. Was it any wonder I always felt excluded? Not only did I not have a mechanical mind, I certainly didn't have a mechanical soul. Why couldn't they take things on face value, why did it have to matter how things worked? I loved the Westerns and the Warships every bit as much as they did, but what made them work left me cold. At the end of the day, these locos were only interesting as part of the scene. On their own, analysed by spotters with X-ray eyes, stripped down and turned back into blueprints, they were as uninspiring as council dustcarts.

Eventually, after taking some obscure freight route, we arrived in Newquay. Not that anyone cared that much. Newquay was just an excuse; even trainspotters have an inkling they ought to make an effort to look normal. It wasn't worth visiting the beach – the prom was slashed by cold drizzle and we had only an hour anyway – so we grabbed some fish and chips and then retreated to the station bar while we waited for the Western to reverse round to the front of the train.

The China Clay beetled its way down another obscure freight-only branch, and when it reached the end we all had to get out. It wasn't compulsory (a few wives and girlfriends always stayed behind to chew toffees) but it would have looked queer for me to stay on the train. The women would have made me feel like an intruder and I'd have been regarded with suspicion by their menfolk. So I got off, but couldn't help feeling oppressed by the pressures of conformity – even in your leisure time you couldn't escape from it. I stood around in the cold mist while the rest of them set up their tripods and took snaps of Western *Fusilier* 1023 trundling up and down the sidings. The driver hooted for the hell of it and each metallic blast from the klaxon was greeted with a loyal cheer.

'Listen to that!' said Jinx.

I couldn't help but listen since the close-proximity hooting had shaken a large ball of wax from my ear.

'Are we getting back on yet?' I asked.

They all stared at me, baffled by my impatience. They were having a whale of a time, but I just hadn't got the same commitment. Cold and wetness I could take; I'd paid my dues in the rain, snow and freezing fog. What was really getting to me was the madness of doing it in company. I was surrounded by faces which were lit by a light I couldn't understand any more. I felt like an imposter. Unlike many of them, I'd never craved the comforts and security of an all-male environment. I had no need to ingratiate myself with smutty jokes or by reciting all 74 Western names in order. In fact, I'd always hated the locker-room mentality. I had this nightmare: I'd rush along the train, slamming open compartment doors, looking for company, someone to talk to about anything – astrology, decorating, politics – anything but trains. But there'd be no one, just these trainspotterish faces, grinning and ballooning out at me like a scene from a bad trip.

Enjoying the railways was a private pleasure, and I did it in my own way. If I wanted to look dreamy, hypnotized by the lovely syncopated rhythm of wheels on the track, I wanted to enjoy the feeling without being interrupted, poked in the ribs by some bloke telling me a story about that night in 1969 when he took a picture of D1037 on a milk train. I'd never minded in the old days – when there were just three or four of us my inner privacy wasn't violated – but this great restless mass of railway enthusiasm was frightening.

I wanted to join in the fun. I was a fan of the Westerns, after all, but there was something troubling me and I couldn't work out what. Then it hit me: there were no kids. Apart from one or two nine-year-olds out for the ride with Dad, the whole 12-coach train was full of grown-ups. Suddenly the weirdness of it got to me (wasn't there an old sci-fi film with the same childless plot?) and I felt quite uneasy. I was more or less the same age as the rest of them, but I didn't feel like one of them at all. It was the grime, the sauce, shinning over fences, putting pennies on the line, the *Just William*ness of trainspotting that had always attracted me. These people had put all that behind them (not that I really expected them to act so daft at their age); they seemed to have reinvented trainspotting as something much more serious.

The trip back was less joyful. We were all in mourning and I suspended my scepticism out of respect for the occasion. How long would it be before any of us got to see a Western again or heard those Maybach engines echoing over the Devon combes? Who'd have thought we'd have been so sad to see diesels go? Here we were, glum and reflective, trying to cheer each other up with stories about sunny days at Exeter and Newton Abbot. They were bloody good engines, people insisted. Why did they have to get rid of them? But they knew the answer already: railways are businesses not theme parks. In any case, the agony was all part of the fun, wasn't it? We knew all along that steam was doomed, and that the Deltics and Warships and Tats would eventually follow them to the scrapyard. Everything ends up as paperclips in the end. This is elegiac end of trainspotting, the bit that tight-lipped trainspotters find so hard to put into words.

They all pretended to be sad. But no one shed any real tears. Sentimentality abounds in the world of railways, but it's so often mawkish and overblown with clichés. When the China Clay Special was finished and Western *Fusilier* gave its passengers a farewell hoot, Jinx and the rest of them simply went home and filed their slides of the occasion and looked around for another bash.

018 Fare-dodging

I've always loved St Pancras for its style, but trainspotting-wise it's a dead loss. Admittedly it gave sanctuary to the faithful Peaks in the sixties and seventies, but those diesel days are now over, and Panky's grandeur is quite out of keeping with its almost suburban function. That lofty roof that everyone loves so much was built to resound with the bark of steamers, and even the phlegmy growlings of diesel engines. But all that's left are the deadly boring commuter trains of the Bed–Pan line. Midland Mainline has its 125s to Sheffield and Nottingham, but they're nothing to shout about either – even if they do boast a fan club with a membership of 850.

Despite all these criticisms, St Pancras is the station I always prefer when I travel home to the Midlands. Never Euston, not if I can help it. Of all the London stations, St Pancras has the most relaxed and homely feel. Despite the bog units and the burger bar, it has catered for the 1990s without sacrificing too much of its essential spirit, unlike Euston and Victoria, which now resemble shopping malls with a few trains somewhere at the back.

It seems like they've been scrubbing the front of St Pancras for nearly a decade. The whole thing is a joke, one of those wild Thatcherite projects, like the Minister for Litter, or Canary Wharf. This restoration has been on and off for so long that the building seems to have had a semi-permanent dressing of scaffolding and green plastic sheeting for years. It must be a decade since the *Evening Standard* had a jokey headline about the 'Return of the Pink Pancras'. And we're still waiting. It will be completely pink again, I tell myself, mainly because I'd love to see it.

There's a story, probably apocryphal, that an American tourist wandered into this wedding cake of a station in the mistaken belief that it was Westminster Abbey.

They don't make stations like St Pancras any more. They just couldn't do it. The last time British Rail built a big station was Milton Keynes Central, a folly which speaks for itself. It's a prime example of eighties' excess; a six-platform station where there's about a million-to-one chance of more than two trains ever stopping there simultaneously. It must have looked great on the drawing-board, with colourful matchstick figures dotting the platform, but no one will ever have a romance on Milton Keynes, it will never be the scene of a Brief Encounter. Come to think of it, I've never seen a trainspotter there either.

I often wonder if my life would have been very different if I'd had a job on the railways. What job could have been better for a railway buff? It would simply have given me plenty of time to look at trains. Being a BR employee wouldn't have been too awful, would it? (Yes, it would. I never could bear taking orders, and especially from the new breed of smug graduates who knew nothing about railways and even less about the brotherhood of railwaymen. So I kept my pride and kept telling myself that fame was just around the corner.)

Yet how much more of my life was I going to fritter away, clumsy booted and grubby fingered, working in a Wellington boot factory? I wrote novels in my head to relieve the boredom and put myself at risk by not looking what I was doing. The money was decent and there were factory girls to flirt with, but I still needed something more.

Greg, my best friend from the hostel, was still at drama school, but he'd moved to a crummy flat above a kebab shop in the King's Cross hinterland. It was the kind of bohemian life I hankered after, and for my fix I often skived off work to get down to London. What fun it was, the pubs and the crazy girls from drama school and the all-night café with the one-armed waitress. Tanked up, drunk on beer and ambition, we'd walk back across London at all hours of the night. Sometimes, passing through King's Cross at 3 a.m. and seeing some slow passenger train waiting to depart, I wanted to grab Greg and take him north, show him what an adventure it could be. But he had drama classes to go to, and I had to find a job somehow if I was to jack it in at the factory and return permanently to London.

Greg and I came from opposite ends of the country and very different cultures. He'd never been a trainspotter and looked on the hobby as some kind of charming Northern eccentricity, like whippet racing or black pudding contests. I'd grown up in the smoky Midlands with its colourful mix of steam and diesel, but Greg came from Sussex, from slap-bang in the middle of BR's most boring region. How could a lad ever have been turned on to trainspotting by the parade of electric bog units that prowled the area, slyly sucking power from the tracks, never showing the slightest evidence of power or temperament. A steamer or a diesel in difficulty always put on a show of emotion, rattling, roaring, whining, erupting with black smog, but those electric trains were inscrutable, smugly efficient and characterless. Even when they did go wrong, they just sat there sulking or juddered yard by yard along the track. Hence I couldn't blame Greg for being totally uninterested in railways. Still, it hadn't stopped us becoming friends. I didn't want to be in the company of trainspotters all the time, and I suspected that he sometimes got sick of all those gushing drama queens.

The trouble was, we acted as if we were already famous, already the celebrated and wealthy actors and writers we wanted to be. One time, in a reckless fit of high-living, I blew all my spare cash in an Italian restaurant in Camden Town. Bloated with pasta and tipsy on amaretto, we floated out into the cold air of NW1, and it was only then I realized I had nothing left for the train fare home (I didn't have a return because I'd hitched down, and I didn't fancy that hassle on the return trip). What the hell, I'd just have to bilk it. British Rail bloody owed me something after all the train fares I'd put into their pocket since 1964.

In all my trainspotting years I'd never been dishonest. OK, I'd got away with paying half fare well past the official cut-off point (we used to kneel down at the ticket office window) and once, when I lost the return half of my ticket to York, I climbed up a drainpipe to get out of the station. But that was more through embarrassment than fear of prosecution. I prided myself as being a seasoned traveller. Losing tickets was the kind of thing that old ladies and dotty professors did. But I'd never been really dishonest; it was against all the unwritten codes of trainspotting.

Trainspotters have always scorned people who aren't railway-wise, sniggering at OAPs who can't read time-tables and people who turn up too late for their trains. The greatest amusement is afforded by those hapless souls who settle down comfortably on a local train to Berkhamsted in the goofy belief that it's the InterCity to Carlisle. How on earth could anyone possibly mistake an AM10 unit for an 87 haulage? But if he despairs at the yokels and the pensioners, the trainspotter despises those who transgress by putting tomatoes in the ashtrays or weeing on the loo seats, and even the second-class ticket-holders who help themselves to the complimentary InterCity magazines intended for first-class passengers. And fare-dodgers, well, they're the lowest of the low, and should be strung up, put in the stocks and exposed to public disdain on the concourse of Euston. There ought to be a specific place, a railway Tyburn between the Sock Shop concession and the Casey Jones stand-up buffet.

That's how guilty I feel about it, even now. I hadn't just broken the law, I'd gone against my own conscience and broken my record as an impeccable passenger. I was a fare-dodger now, one of those people depicted on the posters as a furtive shadow, a dodger who could never dodge the arm of the law in its officially striped sleeve. As a child who believed that even litter louts would probably end up in the dock, this was totally out of character for me.

So there I sat, spiritually miserable, quite unable to enjoy one bit of the journey. But as each mile passed and we got nearer home, I started to get more optimistic. Maybe I was going to get away with it after all. There's an element of pride in the simplest crime if it's successful. Then the door at the end of the carriage slid open and the ticket inspector appeared.

I'd rehearsed my story, just in case, but I was so panicked I got mixed up. Would I say the ticket was simply lost, or claim it had been snatched from me by a mugger? The inspector was just an ordinary guy with a pair of clippers in his hand, but he might as well have been a South African secret policeman flexing his bullwhip for all the fear he put in me. All those memories of Stewarts Lane came flooding back. How bloody and unfair it was when I so wanted to be friends with the railways. Perhaps if I told him how faithful I'd been, how I used to sit on the wall and wave to drivers and guards . . . But no, all he'd see was just another fare-dodger trying it on. Why had I done it? I'd rather have walked back from London to the Midlands than go through this torture.

As he got nearer and nearer I thought I might be sick with fear. But then there was a delay, an old lady asking some long-winded question about connections. I was busy praying, but I did notice we were slowing down, coming into Leicester. Eventually he clipped the old lady's ticket and moved on towards me. And then, with a screech and a jerk, the train stopped in the station. The ticket inspector heaved a sigh, shot a glance at the remaining half a dozen passengers, then jumped off. His shift had ended at Leicester, and I'd had the closest shave of my train-travelling life. I was giggling with relief, scarcely able to believe my luck.

The memory of that journey has never quite vanished. In later years, when I was better off, I was able to enter the grand station with a fat wallet under my jacket. But I never shook off the guilt entirely. To this day I always clutch my ticket fiercely, and even then I have to take it out and check it every ten minutes. I have this nightmare that when the ticket inspector turns up I'll blithely whip it out of my pocket, only to find that I've been clutching a 20p Persil voucher.

019 A New Agenda

In December 1978 Greg was in a pantomime in Worthing and, having nothing better to do, I went down to stay with him in the small flat he'd rented near the station. I'd always wanted to live somewhere overlooking the railway. Anywhere would have done, anywhere except the Southern region. The weathermen said it was the coldest winter since 1962, but even snow couldn't lend those electric bog units any charm.

We spent New Year's Eve in a little backstreet pub.

Greg went off with some actress and I drank in the New Year on my own. After some New Year kisses (but no promise of anything else) I lurched out into the sharp air of 1979 and staggered home, using the gleaming railway tracks as a guide. I had no idea then that it would be a year of changes.

Back in Belsize Park I got a job in the local pub and managed to get myself a life. Trainspotting hardly figured in my thoughts any longer. I wanted to be a writer and I didn't think that writing and trainspotting could comfortably co-exist in the same head. There was just too much paperwork involved. Still, even if I no longer walked around with pen at the ready to jot down numbers, I wasn't impervious to the railways.

Jinx was still working at Burton station and I always stopped for a quick chat whenever I got off the train on my weekends home. But Belsize Park and Burton-on-Trent were different planets. We had trains in common, of course, but whenever I asked him what was going on on the railways, I felt as if he was talking in a foreign language. All kinds of nicknames seemed to have been invented and I didn't dare show my ignorance by asking for a translation. There was a new agenda too. Sitting at the lineside jotting down numbers was out of favour, 'bashing' was the order of the day now, riding up and down the lines and trying to accumulate a set amount of 'mileage' behind each loco. One thousand miles of haulage behind every Peak or Hoover, for instance.

To compensate for losing touch, I began to feel nostalgic. I was pleased to see how much of the past still remained. The old steam sheds were still standing (a local firm had taken them over for use as a warehouse) and on a Sunday afternoon I'd walk down the path from Steamer Gates and have a look around. The little door was bricked-up with breeze blocks, so I couldn't go inside, but walking through the yard and looking up at the smashed and soot-blackened windows I could easily travel back fifteen years. Rumour had it that some railwaymen buried half a dozen Jubilee nameplates in the shed yard, intending to recover them later and sell them, but then they'd gone and forgotten the exact location. I knew it was just another treasure story, but I couldn't help wondering, as I crunched across the ancient clinker, if those nameplates were really buried inches beneath my feet, the brass still perfect beneath its coating of verdigris. I did find a couple of pages from a *Daily Sketch* of 1967, though, yellowed and oily but still readable. There was an article about Twiggy, and I pictured one of the old train drivers reading it during his break and laughing: 'Skinny bit of a kid. Don't they make lasses with any meat on 'em any more?' But maybe he knew then that the future belonged to skinny girls in mini-skirts and not bristly men in overalls.

The footbridge at Wetmore Sidings was still there too, though the signal box was derelict. I was able to walk up the steps and take a look inside. How strange it was to find all these citadels and control centres deserted and in ruins, and to walk in, like a soldier sweeping an abandoned kingdom. After all my carefree trespassing when the railways were working, this felt quite wrong. Anyway there was nothing worth nicking. Every bit of scrap metal and possible souvenir had been removed. Devoid of importance, the vandals had soon got to work on it. It was now little more than a shed full of broken glass, far too empty and windswept to harbour ghosts.

This kind of nostalgia had no charms for Jinx. He was too busy chasing Peaks up and down the St Pancras–Derby line and building up his collection of colour slides. I think Andy, who'd always been closer to the poetic side of trainspotting, would have understood how I felt, but I hadn't seen him for ages. He was out of town. I'd heard on the grapevine that he'd gone to Spain to teach English. He'd split up with Lynn and had found someone a bit more down-to-earth. Pipsqueak was still on the scene, but he'd changed his name to Lord Fishfinger and was trying to get a band together. I wasn't

Desolation – both physical and emotional. The old signal
box at Wetmore Sidings

sure whether he'd want to talk about the old days.

Burton-on-Trent was changing beyond recognition,
and for the first time I could see how much the railway
had defined the town I'd grown up in. It had split it
right down the middle. All the big factories gathered
close to the railway as well, so it was no coincidence that
the posher you were the further away you could get from
all that racket and muck and hard slog. No one had ever

chosen to live close by the railway. But now, with all the clutter and activity of the old railway scene vanished, those small houses at Little Burton Bridges looked high and dry and twice as mean. No doubt the people who lived there were grateful for the silence at nights and the chance to hang their washing out, but at the same time it exposed their poverty to the public gaze. They looked a bit like people on a reservation, as if they didn't belong to our decade at all.

But if I'd mothballed my trainspotting books, it didn't mean that my love affair with the railways was over. Far from it.

The Eighties

020 A Grey Train to Fontainebleau

The grand railway hotels were a bit before my time, and they would have been out of my price range anyway. But I do have fond memories of a weekend in the Café de la Gare at Fontainebleau.

1979 had lived up to its New Year promise. While the snow was still on the ground, I had my first article accepted by the *Observer* and got friendly with a Camel-smoking French girl called Marie-Christine. We had a fun few months, but I knew she wasn't in London for ever. One day a man in a white shirt came to the Belsize Tavern and took 'Je T'aime Moi Non Plus' off the juke-box, and it seemed like just the next day she was on her way home. I kept playing The Rolling Stones' 'Love In Vain' over and over on our crummy record player, and when it came to the bit where Mick sings 'I followed her to the station . . .' I blubbered like an orphaned seal pup. Stations, which had always held the promise of an open door, were now places where that same door got slammed in your face. For the first time I was forced to look at them as a scene of departures and farewells.

But when Marie-Christine invited me over for the August Bank Holiday weekend I jumped at the chance. The station was a place of hope again.

Mind you I'd become quite blasé about the London–Paris trip, and the Gare de Lyon, once so enchanting, was as familiar as Euston or Derby. But I was on a promise and it made the journey a pleasure: rattling through the Paris suburbs on the grey train to Fontainebleau, warmed by the sun and soundtracked by Jean-Michel Jarre. (Provence may be an old-timer with a beret and an accordion, but Paris is romantic-techno and Jean-Michel has it off to a T.) I even had the chutzpah to pass myself off as native and, on being thanked for a light, waved off the favour with a cheerful 'De rien.'

Marie-Christine hadn't bothered to fix up any accommodation. When I arrived she simply marched into the Café de la Gare opposite Fontainebleau station and asked the patron for a room. He stopped drying his Ricard glasses and tossed her the key. Eight pounds a night for a love-nest – who could complain? It had a fluffy double bed, a view across the railway, and, being on the first floor, was close enough to the café terrace for us to earwig everyone's chat. If I'd wanted to I could have chucked peanuts in the old men's wineglasses. Lying in bed listening to the railways sing and chatter is one of the most comforting feelings I know. Unlike the screeching cars and roaring motorbikes that frighten us from sleep, passing trains fit in easily with the rhythms of nature. In Britain or France or Finland, it's as if you're listening to the same tide wherever you are.

Readers might be forgiven for expecting a funny story here. You know the kind of thing: how Marie-Christine lay naked on the bed while I leaned out of the window taking snapshots of a BB16000 trundling through the station with a trainload of mustard from Dijon. But I wasn't that easily distracted. Trains may make an ideal displacement activity for middle-aged men stuck in boring marriages, but for anyone with his eight pints of blood left, trainspotting must always take second place.

Still, with the regular swish and clatter of trains, I couldn't completely forget that the railway was there. During the day, when Marie-Christine had to work (she was at a summer camp for French kids), I was left alone to wander through the woods and find myself an eyrie overlooking the track. I wonder if it gave passengers a creepy shock, as they admired the greeny-gold forestry, to suddenly see a lone figure sitting watching them, just like one of those loiterers they talk about on *Crimewatch*: 'It may well be that the man was an innocent trainspotter and if he comes forward we can eliminate him from our inquiries . . .'

Just as I adored Marie-Christine's accent (even her swearing sounded sexy), she loved my Englishness and the sound of me talking. It didn't matter about what, any nonsense would do. I only had to say 'snug as a bug in a rug' to get her giggling and, for all I know, my ramblings about the golden days of British Railways probably sounded dead romantic to her. How could she have understood anyway? 'I had a love affair with steam' has no true translation into a non-trainspotting culture. Taken literally it sounds truly surreal, and it makes me laugh now to imagine what she thought I meant.

On the Saturday evening we took the local train back into Paris. A Jacques Tati film at a cinema in the rue Mouffetard was followed by dinner in a boisterous little Greek place. Hand in hand, we strolled back across the Pont d'Austerlitz to the Gare de Lyon, where the faithful little local train was humming away to itself at the platform. It was well past midnight and it looked as if we'd be the only people on it. Cheered by a good meal, warmed through by pastis, we could sit and cuddle for half an hour. But that wasn't to be. A couple of soldiers got on, then two more. Hearing shouts, I looked out of the window and saw dozens more stampeding down the platform – it looked like an entire battalion. Soon every seat and squatting space was taken. We felt as if we'd been caught up in a mobilization. But these were conscripts with no reason to be proud of their military status. They just wanted a good piss-up and a laugh before they got back to the camp routine.

Puffing on their Gauloises (it would have been suicide to point out that it was a No Smoking compartment) and swigging their beers, the squaddies stared at us with bleary-eyed hostility. We were the only civilians on the train, and Marie-Christine was the only woman. Who the hell did I think I was, taking one of their women? This is it, I thought. They'll knife me and throw me from the train, then they'll rape Marie-Christine. They probably hadn't had a woman for months. I tried to keep my cool, since I felt it would only take one wrong glance to trigger the nightmare.

One by one the suburban stations came and went: Villeneuve-St Georges – Yerres – Boussy-St Antoine – Combs-la Ville Quincy. I didn't fancy being buried in any of these suburbs. How would my mum ever get to visit my grave if she couldn't even pronounce the name of the bloody station? The journey was only forty minutes, but every second was agony. I looked at the floor mostly, but I remember the smell even now – Gauloises, beery belches, the hum of unwashed male flesh. But at last we slowed down and I was relieved to recognize the approach to Fontainebleau. As we got up to get near the doors I expected our way to be barred at any moment by a tattooed arm, but politely they all shuffled their feet aside to make a gangway for us. They even wished Marie-Christine goodnight and gave me a conspiratorial wink. So much for paranoia.

It was only a long weekend, but I went home on top of the world. Two months later I gave up my half of the flat I shared with Greg and set off to live in France full-time. Marie-Christine had sorted out a flat for us and I was full of youthful fervour. I would get a dishwashing job to support myself and write my novel. Blinded by love I didn't even think how ridiculous I must have looked as I struggled down to Victoria with a suitcase, a bag, a typewriter, and a heavy pile of LPs.

But I knew something was wrong as soon as Marie-Christine met me at the station in Besançon. The twinkle in her eyes had gone and I quickly detected a shiftiness to her. But it wasn't another man, it was another girl. In between the Bank Holiday idyll in the Café de la Gare and my arrival in Besançon, an old crush of hers had turned up on the scene and it had quickly developed into a full-blown affair. There was no place for a man, and though I stuck it out bravely for a month in the hope that she'd change her mind, I was totally frozen out.

One evening we drove over to Dijon to see Lou Reed in concert. Lou was obviously in a bad mood, with nothing but two-fingered contempt for those faithful fans who called on him to do old favourites. But he did agree to do 'Walk On The Wild Side'. The audience was loving it, and so was I, until a thought struck me. There were no beautiful black girls at the mike, so who would do the shivers-up-the-back 'do-be-do-be-do' bit? I soon found out. Step forward three burly and half-drunk roadies. The illusion was shattered. The world was turned upside down. You couldn't even rely on the old songs for comfort any more.

The next day I was on the train back to London, tail between my legs. I'd had to borrow the train fare off Marie-Christine but she'd willingly stumped up, glad to see me go. Not that she hated me, it was more that she was overcome with guilt.

Staring into space, fidgeting on the plasticky seats, all I could think of was Marie-Christine and what a fool I'd made of myself. And all the while I kept seeing these three fat gits stepping up to the mike, turning my misery into some kind of camp singalong.

What has all this self-pity, however justified, got to do with trainspotting? Maybe very little, maybe everything. I know for sure that if I'd had to go home by road, I'd have been totally numb. All that concrete and those motorway lights would have alienated me beyond recall, like a burnt-out case from a Jean-Luc Godard movie. Though I could hardly have been more traumatized just then, the trains kept me sane, cocooned in safety, tied securely to home by those ribbons of steel. Inch by inch they would pull me safely home, through Paris and Boulogne and the endless suburbs of south London, all the way to the Tube station at Belsize Park.

021   East Germany: Steam Days Again

I'd always envied Jinx's travel perks – 75 per cent dis-
counts and an annual quota of free tickets. Not just any
free tickets, either. The way it worked he was quite at
liberty to use his Burton to London returns via Bristol,
Crewe, Carlisle and Newcastle. Yet these privileges were
the rewards of conformity, and I couldn't sell my soul
in return for free travel, however tempting it was. In the
end, though, I found a way of getting my own freebies.

After my railroving article appeared in the *Observer*, I
was inundated with offers of free railway tickets, coyly
referred to as 'travel facilities', from the Swiss, Italian
and German tourist people. One small problem, though.
I was on the dole. The freedom of Switzerland was all
very fine, but how did I get there in the first place, and
what did I use for spending money? Not only that, any
visit would have to be slotted in between signing-on days
at the Camden Town Job Centre.

I thought they'd be able to sort out the getting there
bit for me, but they couldn't even do that. It involved
all kinds of inter-railway dealings and politics that
seemed to date back to the Second World War. British
Rail were prepared to give me a ticket to Dover, and the
Dutch a ticket as far as the German border. But who
would pay the ferryman? That was the slightly surreal
nub of the problem. No one wanted to pick up the tab.

Perhaps if I'd explained my situation to them . . . But
I couldn't. I dreaded them finding out that their Sunday
qualities' travel writer was a claimant with frayed shoe-
laces and £1.47 in his savings book. So, for the price of
a ferry fare, the wonderful basket of freebies slipped
through my grasp.

A year later, when I had more money, I wrote back
to the Swiss Tourist Office and said yes, I'd like an

Alpine railrover ticket, after all. But my fame had evaporated by then. They couldn't remember who I was. Luckily the Germans had better memories and were happy to give me a free rover, and a first class one too.

By that time I had more or less forgotten why I'd wanted to go in the first place. The truth was, I hadn't. Germany had never tempted me and it certainly didn't have the same allure as France. I went partly because it was free, and partly for the trainspotterish urge to add some European place names to my collection. At one time I underlined all the cities I'd visited (Paris, Stockholm, Helsinki, Copenhagen) in my giant Reader's Digest atlas. Now I had a chance to add Hamburg, Munich and Baden-Baden to the list. It sounds pathetic, the worst kind of reason for travel and exactly the kind of thing that gives trainspotters a bad name (I'd originally thought of working my way through Europe alphabetically, all the way from Aalsmeer to Zagreb), but it was only the act of underlining things that may have been a bit odd. I wasn't that different to anyone else, really. Mankind is a collecting animal, and the compulsion manifests itself in scores of ways. Kids collect bubblegum cards; men travel hundreds of miles to obscure football grounds just to say they've been; cooks fill pinewood racks with herb jars, even though they'll never use more than five of them. Consumerism is loaded with 'trainspotting' overtones – the must-have item, the desire for a complete range, whether it be PG Tips cards or kitchen utensils or 'Great Composers' cassettes. The urge to collect, to tick off, to underline, to have the 'full set' is in us all. Anthropologists theorize about parallels with man the hunter, but I incline towards the *Waiting For Godot* theory: trainspotting, like collecting Schwartz spice jars, is just an amusing way of passing an otherwise awesome stretch of time.

If I had to find a 'normal' reason for visiting Germany, it was the chance to see Berlin. The Iron Curtain was still in place and, despite McDonald's having set up shop,

I still saw Berlin as the capital of Cold War intrigue. There was always the possibility that a woman in a Burberry mac might step out of the shadows with a poisoned hat-pin. Ridiculous, I know, but aren't these the kind of mad fantasies which compel us to travel? We all want to get lost in the alleyways behind the souk, don't we? Maybe not. Perhaps the real reason for going to Berlin was simply to say that I'd been. It might even merit a double underlining in the atlas.

The Hamburg–Berlin train was an East German one, green and drab, the perfect vehicle for a nervous peep behind the Iron Curtain. I was travelling first class, but Warsaw Pact first class was worse than our second. Dismally decorated, hard on the bum and stinking of wet dog-ends where melted snow had leaked through the window frames and trickled into the ashtrays, if it wasn't for the figure 1 on your ticket you'd never have known this was first. Still, uncomfortable as I was, the socialist in me had to admit it was a superb trick to play on visitors from the West. They paid extra into the communist coffers in the hope of dodging the rough stuff, but they got a salutary taste of austerity instead. God knows what the second class was like.

Our train squealed to a halt at the border-post and the guards got on, tramping down the corridor, kicking the dusty snow off their boots. The Alsatians snarled at the scent of Western wealth and my heart thumped with apprehension. What if there was something wrong with my visa or they simply didn't like the self-satisfied British smirk in my passport? I'd joked about it back home, but I really did fear that I might be taken off the train and never seen again, just like the old dear in *The Lady Vanishes*. My body would be found by picnickers who'd wonder why my trousers were missing, while an off-duty soldier in Leipzig would be wowwing the girls with his trendy Levi's. I was thinking of fingering my name on the misted-up window, just in case, when in they walked, slamming the compartment door open with well-practised menace. I fumbled for my documents and smiled at them hopefully.

In the event the two guards were as polite as cucumber sandwiches (unlike the British immigration officers who hadn't given anyone a smile). Even the growling dogs turned out to be more like Gnasher from the *Beano*, and looked hopefully at each passenger for some tit-bit. I couldn't help thinking that the Cold War pantomime was all a show for the tourists, and I wouldn't have been surprised if they'd passed round the hat.

Brown and frozen and lifeless, the East German scenery was as dull as everyone had warned me it would be. Then, suddenly, I had a shock. A familiar hiss, a cloud of steam and smoke flattened itself against the windows, and through it, like the clearing mist of a dream, I caught sight of an old steam engine. I was mesmerized. The past – my past – still existed here. They'd changed the station names and the sign for the Gents, but I could have been somewhere in Yorkshire in 1966, with a steam train hissing impatiently by the water tower, railwaymen with greasy overalls and cigarettes bobbing on their lips. The simple black and whiteness of this image left me with a dull ache in my heart, but I had to fight the urge to stick my head out of the window for a closer look. This snow wasn't the soft and fairylike stuff you got on Christmas cards, but splintery needles of ice which danced in angry gusts and drove themselves into the jelly of your eyes. In any case, I had to remember we were behind the Iron Curtain, and I'd read enough scare stories about trainspotters being arrested by the secret police for spying.

I felt disappointed, and reluctant to let this vision slip away from me. But I wasn't obsessed enough about trains to risk hypothermia, or imprisonment. Anyway, what did they mean to me, these odd European steamers with half of their insides on the outside? They were hardly in the same class as Castles or Britannias, so I didn't feel as if I owed them any loyalty. For me to be truly hooked there had to be more, really, than the simple fact that they were steam engines. So I stayed huddled in my seat until the concrete wall closed in around us and funnelled our train through the fog-shrouded suburbs of Berlin.

Behind the Curtain. A Polish 2–8–2 at Lublin during an evening rush hour in the seventies

You wouldn't want to see my snaps. There's the obligatory snap of Checkpoint Charlie, of course, but why the hell did I take a picture of a railway yard covered in snow? There weren't even any engines at work there; it was just a frozen fan of lines, a photograph of meaningless idleness, titled 'Berlin Marshalling Yard Featuring No One'. I can't even imagine how I ended up there when I should have been frowsting in a café on the Kurfürstendamm, having a coffee and a bratwurst and keeping myself warm. Instead I'd wandered off the beaten track and found myself standing on a railway footbridge with ice biting into my toenails.

After a week, I was glad to be heading back home. My abiding memory of Germany was of the icy draughts that left tears in my eyes. I was the trainspotter who came in from the cold. And the *Observer* had expressed provisional interest in a piece about the trip. So I wouldn't be a journalistic one-hit wonder. At this rate I could see myself with a brilliant career as a travel writer.

022   Love on a Very Short Branch Line

Most weekends in the early eighties the train from Paddington to Henley-on-Thames was a regular trip. These were delightful days. I was young, I had my first Barclaycard, and I was in love with an English rose. Elaine was the kind of woman I'd always dreamed of meeting. As well as having big brown eyes she'd been to a boarding school where everyone wore straw hats and went home at weekends to a Home-Counties semi with two bathrooms and two giggling sisters. This was the daydream I'd had since I was a kid collecting steam numbers, an erotic and suspiciously snobby fantasy that had helped fill the gaps between trains.

Trainspotting was definitely on hold. For one thing, I was used to London and didn't need trains as friends in the same way as I had. And I'd got so many of the numbers now, whole sets of Peaks and Deltics. I'd jot down a number if I saw one, but I couldn't be bothered with the time and expense of chasing around the country after the few I still needed. Well, those were my excuses. The ultimate truth was that I'd fallen head over heels. Elaine was pretty and polite, loyal and educated. She could recite the opening passage of Kafka's 'Metamorphosis' in German and, kissed to me in her sweet Southern twang, it made me roll over like a pussycat. I never thought I'd meet anyone who could make an existential nightmare sound like an invitation to make love in a warm shower.

Hold on, I hear cynics saying, let's run through this

again. The guy was a trainspotter, then he meets a nice girl and suddenly decides that trains aren't so interesting, after all. Isn't that proof enough for the nerd theory, that trainspotting is a displacement activity for sad sexless men?

I don't think Elaine cared about trainspotting one way or the other, really, but she certainly didn't think there was any stigma attached. One of the 'character references' I used when I first met her was my *Observer* piece about railroving, copies of which I'd been carrying around for just such an opportunity. I'm not saying it mesmerized her, but it was at least original, and I like to think it lent me a touch of glamour. If I called myself a trainspotter (and there was no reason to keep it hidden), I wasn't a balding bore haunting the platforms of Clapham Junction, but a young guy with a passport full of smudged border stamps, and ambitions to be a journalist.

I'd never been to Paddington in my early spotting days and it had lost its crackle and mystique by the time I did. But even in 1980, with honking taxis, the rattle of parcels trucks, and old ladies staring anxiously at the clattering indicator boards, it could still deliver that big-station atmosphere. I'd always thought of Paddington as a benevolent kind of station. There were none of the rent boys, prostitutes and runaways you found at other London termini. Whereas Euston could only offer you boring destinations like Birmingham or Coventry, Liverpool Street was for Essex people, and Victoria merely suburban, Paddington was a holiday station full of promises, the place you came to when you wanted a train for Teignmouth, Paignton or Newquay. The Tannoy crackled out its litany of a forgotten England: '. . . calling at Saltash, Liskeard, Lostwithiel, Par, St Austell . . .' Hypnotized, something in your genes awoken, you just wanted to walk up to the waiting train and go. Arriving in Penzance, you could walk out of the station and there'd be no more cities, just the sea and the sky.

A Hoover Class 50 at Paddington in the early eighties

But I could only look with envy at the passengers who were going that way. For Elaine and I it was a routine trip, sneaking away from one of the suburban platforms on a bog unit stinking of diesel and fag smoke. I loved being with Elaine, but I was always wishing we were doing something more crazy, like running off to Paris, or something.

There's an old piano-and-whimsy song by Flanders and Swann, 'The Slow Train', which evokes a picture of England at its most leisurely and bucolic. Sheer bunkum! We've always been two-faced about our railways. We insist we still miss the old puffers and third-class compartments, lazy porters and cheery drivers. It's a falsified memory that lies behind our contradictory attitude to railways: it's why we tut and smirk and guffaw when the first-ever Eurostar is late or trains are stopped for the wrong kind of snow. These are trivial matters, but they push wars and famine and even Lady Di off the front page. The jokes are filed away in the national joke archive to be used for the next fifty years. 'They don't know how to run railways any more,' grumble people who've never been on a train for twenty years and couldn't even tell you when steam stopped. But they all claim allegiance to the myth of the branch line and the Slow Train.

In fact, there's nothing more boring than the combination of branch line and slow train. It's just about tolerable when you go abroad; on holiday you get to see every little station as a postcard view, a sleepy halt full of local characters. Or that's how memory reinvents it. But there's nothing fascinating about Westbourne Park or Acton, no glamour in Southall or Hayes & Harlington (though I suppose these same names sound odd and exotic to InterRailers from Madrid or Munich, who for years have probably cherished fond memories of the sunny afternoon their train stopped at West Drayton and an old man with a straw hat asked them the time).

To get to Henley we had to change at Twyford. The branch line experience is something else that has been almost written out of British life. Up until Beeching went on the rampage with his axe, there were hundreds of branches and numerous twigs. The railway map of Britain was endlessly fascinating, like an organic growth. But if it looked random, it had a beautiful logic. It filtered passengers from the grandest of London stations, through its country junctions, delivering them right into the heart of the cutest village or quietest market town. The branch line is one of those rural fantasies that refuses to die, as English as Elgar or sweet shops. Little wonder then that Edward Thomas' 'Adlestrop' is one of our favourite poems, and that the book, *The Country Branch Line*, with its watercolour pictures, is one of the bestselling railway titles ever. Since branch lines are a dead loss for trainspotting, one can only assume that its main readership is amongst the kind of people who spend their weekends buying grandfather clocks and spinning wheels.

Not that Henley branch was one of the archetypes. It's quite small in fact, with only two stops along the way, Shiplake and Wargrave, each one a flyblown memorial to the golden days. What was once busy enough to provide a living for a stationmaster and his minions is now just an elegant ruin. Today, with no minions, let alone a stationmaster, and only rudimentary buildings to shelter the travellers, the branch line stations of Olde England make perfect dens for teenagers to snog, smoke dope or swig Strongbow from two-litre bottles. And if anyone has a felt-tip to leave their name behind, so much the better.

Elaine's mum approved of me anyway. I don't know if she'd been fearing the worst, but now she could see that I wasn't a punk or a claimant, and I wasn't into smack or fascism. I had a nice M&S jacket and I helped with the washing-up. Trainspotters were just as capable of getting a precious daughter pregnant, of course, but at least they could be relied on to make safe if uninspiring son-in-laws. Trainspotting was a badge of normality in a changing world.

I wonder how many young girls would be happy to take on a spotter as a boyfriend now. Few of them actually know any in their own age group. The only trainspotters they know are the stand-up comic's stereotype, and perhaps their fathers. It's an old guy's pastime. And what girl wants a fella with the same interests (and the same ill-fitting jeans) as Dad? I've seen girls sniggering at the slow antics of trainspotters. After so many years of media mockery, it's a definite no-no. If I were still in my hot flush of youth, I don't think I would mention my 'hobby'.

Elaine remembered steam trains. She'd been brought up in Malaya, one of those countries where old steamers could still be found working the rubber plantations. I was intrigued. There were always tales circulating about old steamers that had been 'borrowed' during the war and never returned. Stupidly, I expected her to have fond memories of it all, but however much I pumped her, she couldn't recall any details. How the hell would she know if the locos were 2–8–2s with tenders or 0–6–0 tanks? They were only part of the foreign backdrop, no more important than the taxis or the stalls that sold stir-fried dog. Talking about the Orient Express or my trip to Berlin was one thing, but she certainly wasn't prepared to entertain me with the details of the 7.35 latex special to Ban Pak Phraek, even if I promised to take her to the Pizza Hut in exchange.

As well as the two sweet sisters, Elaine had a kid brother too. He was a spotter, but his stomping ground was Heathrow Airport, training his binoculars on the jumbos and airbuses as they shot off over the Hounslow rooftops. Not my cup of tea at all. Spotters do have an affinity with each other, but it's not total. Of course we understand the need to spot, the thrill of the spotting itself and the satisfaction involved in the paperwork, but that's as far as it goes. Despite an invitation to try, I could no more get interested in plane-spotting than I could in decorative pokerwork or jam-making.

We always had a bog unit on our way to Henley, but on Sunday nights, when Elaine's dad gave us a lift to Reading, we always managed to pick up a fast train back to Paddington, as often as not one of the HSTs which were now quite common. They'd been a novelty at first and we were charmed by the gadgetry; you could walk along the carriage with your coffee and sandwiches and the doors would swish open like magic. They could even make you a bacon butty in their fully equipped buffets. But these Flying Bananas were taking over all those long-distance trains that had once been hauled by Westerns and Hoovers. We'd surrendered all the romance of travel for the simpleton's excitement of a sliding door. It was a bad bargain, and it made the future all too obvious.

023 'Return to Athens, Please'

What on earth made me want to go all the way to Athens by train anyway? Adventure, bloody-mindedness, a chance for some exotic trainspotting? A bit of each, I suppose. But there was another reason. A girl I'd once fancied was working in a bar down there, and it only took an innocent letter from her to revive an old obsession. I was fed up with life in an office, and this sudden chance of travel and adventure made the nine-to-five routine all the more awful. For once I stood up for myself. If they wanted me to stay, I told them, I wanted a raise and two weeks' holiday to recover my *joie de vivre*. To my surprise they agreed. I wrote and warned Suzanne I was on my way. The next day I went to get my ticket to Athens. This was a wildly eccentric request, or so it seemed from the way the ticket clerks stared at me through their little glass window.

'Return to Athens, please.'

'Ashford, sir? You want the Suburban window.'

'No, Athens. In Greece.'

What followed was like a scene from an old comedy. They had to blow the dust off rarely used manuals and then, still unsure, ring their superiors for advice. I got my ticket eventually, but lost all claim to normality. Yes, of course I was a nutter. Why else would I go all that way by train? Not only did it cost nearly three times as much as going by air, it also took twenty times as long.

Elaine came to Charing Cross to see me off on the 13.00 to Boulogne. I kept asking her if she minded me going, but she said no. We'd been sharing a single bed for two years and perhaps she was glad of a chance to turn over. Still, I watched with regret as she walked back to the Underground. I knew quite well that I was being

177

a deceitful little shit, but the sense of adventure soon reasserted itself. I bought a *Times*, a *Punch* and a *Railway World* from W. H. Smith and settled down in my seat. Further along the carriage were one or two couples on their way to Paris for a romantic weekend. I envied them and felt doubly guilty. I could have used all that money to have a weekend in Paris with Elaine. At the same time I longed for an excuse to say, 'Me? I'm going to Athens, actually.'

At the Gare de Lyon I fortified myself with a hot dog and a beer, then bought a clutch of Kronenbourg cans and boarded the overnight train for Venice. I'd booked a couchette, so even though I had to share with an old guy who kept switching on his reading light and counting his coins, I did manage to get a good night's sleep. So good, in fact, that I snoozed all the way through Switzerland without noticing it and woke up below the green hills of Lombardy.

Venice! One of those places everyone wants to go to, but merely a junction for me, a place to change trains. I have a quick look round the muddy canals and scabrous houses for politeness' sake, but my main intention is to get something to eat.

The next morning I'm behind the Iron Curtain, and further away from home than I've ever been before. As the train of drab green carriages snakes into Belgrade station I catch sight of some steam engines. Not prettified blue-painted antiques, but dirty workhorses banging trucks together in the station sidings, leaking steam and wheezing. As the train squeals to a halt in the terminus I jump off and run back to the end of the platform with my camera.

Suddenly there's a machine-gun pointing up my nose and I swivel round to see some kind of official shaking his head. The message is obvious, but even with a gun pointing at me I'm tempted to say, 'Oh yes, my Ministry of Defence is really interested in your old shunting engines,' though I resist the temptation. I snap the lens cap back on my camera and sit down on a luggage trolley, contenting myself by watching.

I'm soon cheered up as I watch the following scene. Our train is being shunted into a new order, having its restaurant car detached and two sleeping cars hooked on. Some American backpackers are filling their water bottles and washing their feet at a tap on the platform. Seeing their train move, they panic.

'Jesus Christ! Tony, the fucking train's going.'

They grab their shoes and water bottles and sprint the length of the platform bare-footed, yelling, screaming, dancing on bits of glass, and hollering as only panicked Americans can. Anyone would think they were after the last helicopter out of Saigon. They collapse on the platform as the carriages disappear from view. One of the girls is crying. She has left her bag and her radio on the train. I suppose I could tell them the train will be back any minute, but I don't. I watch them, shamefully amused by their distress. Two minutes later the train reappears from beyond the station. Tony lights up a Marlboro and laughs.

'Jesus Christ! Tony, the fucking train's coming back.' Mary dries her tears. Their relief is childlike and touching, and I can't help wondering why the Americans let such innocents venture abroad.

I haven't eaten a thing since we left Venice, so when the train stops at Niš for twenty minutes, I get off in search of refreshment. Beer bottles are recognizable anywhere, so pointing is enough to make my desires known to the lady at the kiosk. The food is more enigmatic, but I see some squares of golden pastry that look quite appetizing. I point at them, flash two fingers at the woman, and she hands them to me wrapped in greaseproof paper. Back on the train I discover that, in the warmth of my hands, the golden pastry is rapidly degenerating back to fat and flour. I bite into one of the squares, and feel like throwing up. It's packed with a block of gristle and mince. There's no way I can eat it, so I throw it out of the window and get stuck into my beers. (I don't feel too guilty about chucking things out of the window since there is a continuous ribbon of litter from Belgrade to the border, a blur of blue, red and yellow that is forever at the edge of your vision.)

After Leskovac I have the compartment more or less to myself. This is the life, nothing to do but read and look out of the window and listen to the reassuring clickety-clack of wheels on track. It's midnight when the train arrives in Thessaloniki. Through the window I see an old lady struggling with her cases and go to help her up the steps. I doze off again and wake up on the outskirts of Athens.

The suburbs of foreign cities, tedious and familiar to their inhabitants, have an exotic quality for the traveller. I'm intrigued by all the pink-painted houses, sleeping shops and early morning bus queues. And more steam engines. Unwanted and rusty in the sidings, but real steamers all the same. I grip the window and stare hopelessly as they dwindle back in the distance. Even dead and rusting they still have a residual fascination. As far away from home as I am, I can't help thinking of some half-remembered day in Manchester or Leeds.

Athens station is a surprise. If I hadn't just come through all those suburbs I wouldn't have thought it was a city station. It's nothing like the noisy canopied sheds of Paris, London or Frankfurt, but is hushed and unhurried enough for a tree to grow at the end of one of the platforms. There are unofficial patches of greenery that would never be allowed at Euston or Amsterdam Central. It's all as charming as a country junction in the fifties. Our newly arrived train gives the place some importance. Apart from that there is only an antique railcar with its engine rattling impatiently.

I draw a veil over my two weeks in Athens. Suffice to say I enjoyed myself, even if I didn't get what I'd hoped for – and it served me right.

I'm glad to be going home. I feel quite sentimental

The almost rural peace of Athens' main station

now and long to be with Elaine again, to tell her how much I love her. (She's really going to believe me after I've left her on her own for two weeks and spent five-hundred quid on a journey to Athens in the hope of getting my leg over.)

At the station I walk the length of the train three times looking for Coach K – but I can't find it. I try asking a railwayman what's going on. I have paid for a couchette, I tell him, and show him my ticket for Coach K. He just shrugs and gabbles some excuse in Greek. The plain fact is that there is no Coach K at all. For some reason it only goes up to J.

Luckily there are a few unreserved seats still empty and I manage to get one in a compartment with a quartet of Americans. Luckily . . . ? I'm trying to get to sleep, but they laugh and chatter all night long. They seem to be having a debate about every single aspect of American culture, from baseball, cars, and *Star Trek*, to pizza toppings. I hate them. First thing in the morning I'm going to find another seat.

After a fitful night's sleep, I wave a secret V-sign at my travelling companions and manage to find a seat further along the train. There's only one other man in the compartment and he gets off soon after. I think I'm doing all right. And I am, until we get further into Yugoslavia. The train stops at every single station. At each one another hundred people crowd on. Rowdy people in a bizarre mix of fashions; the men in rough jackets and workboots, or 1970s suits, the women either demure in black headscarves or somehow tarty in Laura Ashley dresses copied on to the cheapest thin material. I'm now sharing a compartment with five young men. They're trying their best to be friendly, but I'd much rather be alone.

'You Anglia?' one of them says.

I nod my head and so trigger a barrage of odd questions.

'You know Crystal Palace?'

'Pink Floyd – bloody good psycho band, huh?'

'You married to sexy English lady?'

The worst thing is that none of them has any notion of personal space. Not only do they keep leaning across me to talk to each other, one of them has now gone to sleep on my shoulder and his garlic breath ripples just inches from my nose.

Someone offers me a slice from some kind of pie. It's suspiciously greasy and has a thumb-print on it, and I think I've been through this before. But I'm hungry and I don't want to risk offending them. I nibble cautiously at the pastry and nod with a lying smile. Then, biting deeper, I gag on a lump of gristle. But I daren't spit it out (for one thing, actually seeing it could make me feel even worse), and for what seems like hours I move the thing around my mouth in an unconvincing mime, not daring to either chew or swallow. Eventually, when the Slavic lads are distracted by something outside the window, I take my chance and cough the mangled lump into a tissue in the hope of chucking it down the toilet later.

I put the grotty food down to the hazards of travelling, but things get worse. I don't know what's going on now, but the lads are getting boisterous. One of them is standing on the seat, straddling his mate and dangling his long fat penis over his head. They laugh uproariously and start bashing each other. I'm totally baffled and disgusted by the smell he has released from his trousers. I don't know whether to laugh at the prank or try to ignore it. It's not just that I don't understand the language, I can't read the unspoken signs either. Are they just messing about, or am I in danger, trapped in a compartment full of gay gang-bangers? For the first time on my trip I'm aware how vulnerable and helpless and far from home I am.

Someone at work tried to sell me a Walkman before I left, but I refused. I wanted real life, I told them, not cassettes. But all this Serbo-Croat babble is getting to me and I'm desperate for the sound of English voices. How grateful I'd be now for one of my Tony Hancock tapes to listen to. I wish I'd stayed with the Yanks when I had the chance. I'd kiss their boots now if only they'd bless me with the sound of their voices. I'll gladly listen to stories about baseball and hamburgers all the way to Paris if I have to.

So now I make my second big mistake. I nod goodbye to the lads and go to try to find the Americans. But the corridors are jam-packed and as stuffy as the rush-hour Tube but without the silence. I can't find the Americans and there's no point in going back, so I end up in a cramped space by the toilets, alternatively standing and squatting on my haunches. And there I am for the next eight hours. I'm jammed close to the door – a door which opens inwards – and every time it opens to let on more passengers my overnight bag is crushed down to the size of a wallet.

Every time a woman goes into the toilet the men in the corridor slip a piece of wire through the door to undo the bolt. The door swings open to expose the poor woman to hoots of laughter. British hooligans often display pretensions of gallantry, but there's no such hypocrisy here.

Crowded as it is, some people manage to grab themselves a pocket of territory – like the two men who've found enough space to spread out a newspaper on the floor and have a meal of stale-looking bread and tinned sardines. But then we stop at a station, and as another hundred people crowd through the door someone kicks the tin of sardines along the corridor, splashing tomato sauce on people's legs and coating the sardines in dust and cigarette ash. There's a right old rumpus and a half-hearted flailing of fists. But the two men manage to recover their sardines and after peeling off the skins deem them fit enough to eat again.

The flush in the toilet isn't working properly, but people still go in, until the shit is brimming over the pan. The smell is overpowering, and I'm beginning to feel almost hysterical with misery. 'Nightmare journey' is an overused cliché, but that's the only description I can think of. The babble of a hundred foreign voices is maddening. I've never been a racist, but I hate these people now, with their dumb rural faces and ugly voices.

The train is far too crowded for the usual passport checks. At Villa Opicina on the border, the Italian authorities make us all get off to have our passports checked. They treat us like scum, yelling and pushing us into line. It's frightening how a pair of boots and a peaked cap can turn a man into a fascist bully. For the first time I feel sorry for these people. Poverty allows them to be treated like rats.

At Trieste the Yugoslavians alight *en masse* to spend their farmers' wages on Western goodies like jeans and Walkmans. A troop of Italian cleaners get on and stuff bin bags with beer bottles, sardine tins, fag packets and banana skins. When they've finished, men in facemasks start hosing down the corridors and drowning the toilets in disinfectant. At least I'm on my own again, and I suppose I should be happy, but the train stinks of carbolic and there's a creepy silence. I imagine this is how the trains must have looked after delivering their frightened passengers to Auschwitz and Dachau.

By the time we get to Venice I'm calm again. I was so fed up for a while that I thought of catching an aeroplane for the first time in my life, just to be back with the people I know. But the panic has passed and I'm sure I can last the twenty-four hours it takes before I'm back in London. Elaine, I'm so sorry. I'll start saving again straight away. I'll take you for a lovely romantic weekend in Paris. We'll have a normal holiday, just like normal couples, just me and you and a little pink hotel on the Left Bank.

024 A Doomed Enterprise: The Sunday Luncheon Special

It was Trish's idea to go on the Sunday Luncheon Special, a steam-hauled train to Stratford-on-Avon with roast beef dinner and high tea included. I doubt if I'd have thought of it on my own. It's not a trainspotter's thing, really, more like one of those show-off ways of spending money and leisure time, like hot-air ballooning or Murder Weekends in country houses.

When you're a trainspotter, mums, aunts and girlfriends think anything to do with railways is a treat, so it's odds on you'll get at least one birthday card with a steam train on it. It's the thought that counts, naturally, but the details always rankle: the card may show the LNER's *Mallard*, and it's useless trying to explain that you're a Great Western man and you've always hated the LNER, and especially *Mallard*, ever since Andy Parker boasted about his grandad seeing it on its record-breaking run. It's a train, and they think you should be happy with it and the fact they've remembered. How should they know the difference between one silly train and another? But that, you want to say but daren't, is the whole point of trainspotting!

Still, there's no point in being churlish, especially if someone else is paying for the Sunday Luncheon tickets. I may as well go along for the crack.

Despite my good intentions, we get off to a bad start anyway. I'm in my usual Millets gear, but Trish has gone and got herself done up like an Edwardian doll – waisted jacket, lacy blouse with a brooch at the throat, hair done up like the Duchess of Duke Street, the whole works. This is just what I dreaded, but before I get chance to tell her off for going over the top, I'm the one who gets it in the neck for being sloppy and boring.

'For God's sake, have you ever heard of anyone going out to dinner in an anorak?'

'What? I thought this was a railway trip?'

As we get off the 159 bus in Ladbroke Grove and walk up to Marylebone station there's a familiar sulphury tang in the air and, as lovable and English as church bells, the cheerful toot of a train whistle. The Bengali greengrocer patiently arranging his satsumas in a pyramid is baffled; they told him Britain had modern railways! But the old-fashioned fuss has galvanized two pensioners. It's as if the whistle has signalled to them across the decades. Old eyes misty with nostalgia, they swap tales of a bygone age busy with troop trains and evacuees fortified by LMSR penny buns.

The station is swarming with steam fans, their bodies festooned with video-cams and tape recorders. They are fully equipped to record their memories and watch them on the home TV later. Who knows, if some unfortunate (preferably a non-trainspotter) gets drenched by a stray fountain of water from the engine there might be a clip worth sending in to Jeremy Beadle.

35028 *Clan Line* basks in the limelight, a gleaming

green leviathan, its wheels and pistons shiny with grease and loving care. I haven't seen this loco since 1967, yet the years in between might as well have never been. The whiff of smoke and hot oil makes me feel a bit queer, yearning for those long-vanished days at Nine Elms and Waterloo. If someone could invent a process to can that special aroma they'd make themselves a fortune from desperate nostalgists like me.

Men forget their wives and mortgages and are children again. They queue patiently to climb up into the driver's cab and listen to tales of gritty times on the iron road.

'Aye, I lost yon fingertip on *The Limited* back in fifty-nine,' the driver tells them. 'Me and Charlie were ten late out of Paddington, so we had to give it some hammer . . .'

The men look fascinated, and then sad as they think, if only I could have been Fred's cheerful stoker instead of going in for financial consultancy. Those who have brought their own children offer them up to be touched by the heroic mutilated hand.

As we pull out of the old Great Central terminus the wheels fight for a grip on the wet rails, and damp woollen steam billows up into the slate-grey skies. We wave to the spotters, but they have no time to wave back, these serious chaps, for a display like this must be photo-graphed and chronicled. Snaking our way across the points, we leave it all behind and plunge into the tunnel under Lord's cricket ground. Flakes of soot swirl in through the open windows. Someone has forgotten to turn the carriage lights on, but the tablecloths have been washed so white we can read our *Sunday Times* in the dazzle.

Breaking daylight again, we rattle past hillocks of mangled cars and the backyards of kebab shops. In one an unshaven cook stands with his first cigarette of the Sabbath, staring at this eccentric intrusion. Dismayed by the city's backside, we gladly hurry on towards the leafy surrounds of Metroland.

Some of the passengers aren't very happy about the soot or the wind, or the clickety-clack. While a couple of trainspotters hang from the open windows with cameras and tape recorders, the rest of the passengers purse their lips in a very British way. They want elegance without soot, they don't want their taste of yesteryear spoiled by trainspotters. When you think of the Orient Express you think of handsome men in white jackets and fancy women with feather boas. There are no loonies on the loose with wirebound notebooks.

Is there going to be a row? You can see people getting excited, this might be fine entertainment! But no, satisfied with his snaps, the spotter slams the window shut and snaps his lens cap back on, blissfully unaware of the spiteful stares. The thing is, unless you actually stick your head out of the window and get a faceful of smoke and coaldust, you don't even know you're on a steam-hauled train. So what's the point? It's a question I've always asked myself. If you can't actually see yourself as that extra in a period drama, you might as well travel on a bog unit with a bag of crisps and a Tango. The biggest thrill belongs to the people who stand and watch the train go by.

Feeling a bit like minor royalty, we sip our tea and wave graciously to our subjects as they lean from their bedroom windows to watch us pass. Further on there's even more spotters. The trip's been well publicized, and some of them have been waiting for ages. Clinging to the sides of bridges or standing in fields of sheep, their zoom lenses peer right in at us. Their wives skulk in the warmth of family hatchbacks which are slowly sinking into the English countryside at its stickiest.

In years gone by it was nothing special to have a meal on a train. Nowadays only businessmen on expenses can afford the prices, so the Sunday Luncheon Special is an indulgence, a chance for Jack and Jill Commuter to cock a snook at the Casey Jones burger and the instant tea which is their normal lot. This is the kind of thing that tired husbands cook up for their wives as a twentieth-wedding-anniversary treat. It's an old con trick in a different format. Hubby gets another look at the old steamers and his wife gets the idea she's being pampered with pink napkins and Piat d'Or.

So far, all's well with the England the passengers are hoping to find; it still has its freckled-faced kids, patient wives and dotty menfolk with harmless hobbies. Now we unfold napkins and prepare for the great British Sunday lunch. Empires were built around our civilized rituals. But, oh dear, this isn't the roast beef of Merrie England. Leathery slices of meat in pale gluey gravy, watery sprouts and seriously underboiled spuds, this is no luncheon to recall the unhurried elegance of trips on The Cheltenham Flyer or The Lakes Express. But, being British, and on a trip all about being British, we suffer it in uncomplaining silence.

Nostalgia's big business these days, and British Rail need the income. But opportunists aren't the best people to trust with your dreams. Young, made-up women in designer uniforms may be what the marketing department think the public wants, but they're no match for those old-time stewards who could balance a spoonful of petits pois at 60 m.p.h.

I hated this Orient Express snobbery, a reconstructed past with a suitable class system. The whole thing was a pose. It had nothing to do with the love of trains at all, but was more concerned with a hankering after the old upstairs–downstairs era. The yuppie years had already seen the re-emergence of shoeshine boys, so it must have seemed quite fitting for people to travel first-class and be served meals by stewards in red waistcoats.

The trouble with nostalgia is that, in the end, it's just a product. Not that British Rail hadn't tried, but they were so intent on getting it right that they'd never succeed, simply because the railways were never quite right in the first place. It was nothing like the real past. Where was Will Hay and his cack-handed crew? Where was the pompous ticket inspector, the bolshy porter, and the fireman who looked like George Formby?

The chaps from the Merchant Navy Preservation Society, who actually own the engine, travel in their own vintage coach and keep the door firmly locked against intruders. They're a bit wary of their passengers. Railway gossip and bloater-paste sandwiches are enough for them. But we aren't train nuts, just daytrippers who'd got the idea off a half-remembered Alan Whicker special.

As we get near Stratford one of the MNPS. stewards, a man in a check jacket, steps into the carriage to address us all, adopting some distinctly CIA-style jargon.

'On termination at Stratford, could we ask you all to de-train as quickly as possible.'

We're going to be terminated, not with extreme prejudice but with kid gloves. The reason for the hurry – and here he coughs apologetically – is some complicated shunting. Shunting is a robust, English word, redolent of childhood nights listening to the clang of buffers in distant goods yards. But it's too raw and rusty for the snobs and the general public. In our car society shunting counts as an obscure technical term, as old-fashioned as haymaking or churning. The steward–owner gropes for some euphemism to make it more acceptable to non-trainspotters. He talks of the 'regrouping of passenger modules', or something like that.

I want to grab him and say, 'Hey, I'm a trainspotter, there's no need to use that fancy language with me.'

But he'd just grin with embarrassed politeness. And perhaps I'm not really a trainspotter any more. I don't feel like one. I'm just another daytripper pretending to be part of High Society, de-training at Stratford.

Call me a philistine, but Stratford is crappy and boring, just another English town cashing in on its cutesy cottages and its family connections. The only thing to be thankful for is that the American tourists have gone home. There's just time for us to buy a bag of Maltesers and visit the superloo.

On our return journey, the twilight turns the windows into dusty mirrors and we glimpse ourselves self-consciously being served with afternoon tea. Far away though it seems, we can hear the well-tempered beat of the locomotive's pistons. The smoke trails out for miles behind us, hanging torn and motionless in the indigo skies over the Home Counties. A mournful whistle scatters the dozing birds in the hedgerows.

We've almost escaped from the 1980s for a few hours, but not quite. Nobody looks that charmed by their trip. They thought by coupling themselves up behind a polished-up steamer they could kid themselves it was 1954 again. But we're so obviously in the 1980s. Looking for the past is a doomed enterprise, and if you have to pay for it you just can't help feeling you've been conned.

025   A Question of Class

The yuppie charades of the mid-eighties tainted us all in one way or another. Like most people with more money than sense, I betrayed my socialist credo by regularly travelling first class between London and Burton.

I'd often sneaked a ride in first class during my teenage trainspotting trips. It was a taste of forbidden fruit – fruit and a mouthful of dust left over from the 1950s. The first-class compartments were defiantly elitist. Instead of the usual greasy roller blinds there were tassled curtains at the windows, and the well-sprung seats were softly padded in regal blue. Sometimes there were even framed pictures of Highland stags or approved landscapes. Everything was imbued with the peculiar smell of old wealth: Parma Violets and old cigars and denture fixative. Passengers' privacy was loyally protected by the ticket inspectors and kids like us weren't even allowed to stand in their corridor, let alone sit down. As we were hustled out of the way, we'd catch glimpses of old brigadiers dribbling in their sleep, ladies living out their last days on a wedge of industrial dividends. They travelled first class for the sake of their old bones, and because it was expected of them.

Today's standard class is comfortable enough for any reasonable human being. First doesn't have that much to offer: travellers get a free magazine and that's about it (and anyone passing through can snatch one from the rack). The premium is not for extra comfort – what really gives the first-class passenger a buzz is the legroom and the status. But it's all open-plan now, and even the smell is breezy and democratic, a haze of Lynx body spray and fresh coffee. There's no style, no mystery, and subsequently the truth is that today's first class is a sad anachronism. We don't really need it or deserve it.

To be honest, I was never at my ease cosseted in all that salmon pinkness. I knew I didn't really belong there. It wasn't any kind of inferiority complex, I just didn't like the idea of first class as a concept. I'd read about the five classes in Imperial Russia and the first-class toilets they'd once had at Waterloo, and I hated it. I could blame that on history, of course, but what the hell were we doing with first and second class in the last bit of the twentieth century?

I enjoyed my anger and spent my journeys examining each of my fellow passengers for signs of snobbery. A combination briefcase, an Armani suit, a guy with the portable phone who was so obviously unimportant he had to resort to ringing out, these people weren't really snobs or aristocrats or TV stars, and that's what disappointed me. They were ordinary men from semi-detached homes who revelled in their own importance.

I nursed a constant fear of ejection. Not because I didn't have the money, but because I wasn't playing the part. Any photographer commissioned to take a snap of first class for a publicity pamphlet would have had to give a wide berth to any carriage I was sitting in. Amongst all the pink-faced stripy-shirted businessmen with their briefcases and Parker pens, I was the worm in the bud. The one with scruffy jeans and trainers, a carrier bag full of newspapers, and a bashed-in Pepsi tin on the table. However much I liked to imagine myself as some kind of fifth columnist, I don't suppose anyone took that much notice of me. It was all a bit silly, really.

My surliness can be traced back to an occasion some years before, when Elaine and I were travelling first class. I was taking her to Burton to meet my mum, so I thought we'd make an occasion of it. We were lounging in our compartment waiting to depart Birmingham when there was a sharp rat-tat-tat on the window. A chubby little red-faced 'railman' glared in at us and jerked his thumb: 'Come on, out of it.'

Elaine and I exchanged glances and decided to ignore him, but a minute later he was back, tapping on the glass. 'I thought I told you to get out of there,' he snarled.

'Why should we?' I demanded, standing up and peering down at him through the open window.

'You're trespassing in first class,' he said, relishing the word 'trespassing'. How lucky he was not to have a lisp.

'We've got first-class tickets.'

He held his chubby hand up towards me. 'Show me.'

'No. You're not a ticket inspector. You're only a porter.'

This slur on his status had him stamping with rage. 'If you don't show me your tickets, I'll have this train blacked. You can explain to the other passengers why they're going nowhere.'

I got out my wallet and mimed an anxious search for our tickets. The delight began to spread across his face. He'd caught two bilkers, he'd get a pat on the back from his supervisor. I drew out the suspense as long as I dared, and felt almost sorry for him when I handed over the two tickets. His face fell and he stuttered his apologies. 'I'm sorry, sir, I really must apologize.'

'S'alright,' I said matily. His subservience embarrassed us. I'd just wanted to travel first class for a change,

I didn't want men tugging their forelocks at me, for God's sake.

'Sorry,' he insisted.

'Forget it.' I sat down with Elaine, anxious to be off on our way.

'It's just that you don't look first class,' he added as the guard blew his whistle and the train drew out.

I'll never know if he was being deliberately sharp or if he'd been so indoctrinated by the class system that he said it quite innocently.

I wasn't that much into trainspotting in the mid-eighties. Since 1976, when I first started travelling between Euston and Birmingham, there'd been little to see anyway. Freed from the compulsion of old habits I began to take more interest in my fellow passengers, and I could always suss out the closet trainspotters. You always get a few of them in first class. They look as if they're perusing office paperwork, then all of a sudden a small wire-

A Class 86 electric setting off with one of the half-hourly Birmingham–Euston trains

bound notebook appears out of their breast pocket and they jot down the number of a Class 87 electric or a shunter, nervously watchful for signs of mockery. Sometimes one of them will improvise a mini confessional with the lid of his briefcase so he can flick through the pages of *Railway Magazine* in peace. Further down the carriage other men browse quite openly through *Mayfair*. They're not ashamed; it's better to have a reputation as a randy executive than be branded a trainspotter.

There was one thing I did notice, though. I kept bumping into *Britannia* and *Royal Scot* and *The Black Prince*. Familiar names, but these weren't the magnificent greenly polished flyers of my childhood. The old names had been hijacked for their nostalgia value and stuck on the side of Class 87 electrics shunting businessmen between Euston and Birmingham. Thirty years before a name would have been something to remark on – 'Look, Dad, Britannia!' Now, nobody cared a toss. It was a wasted exercise.

Another thing that has come to figure significantly in the first-class snobbery is the railway breakfast. Occasionally I had to visit Durham on business, seat paid for, food on expenses, and I treated myself to such breakfasts. The eagerness with which my fellow diners got stuck in was quite touching. From their waistlines it was easy to guess that their wives normally kept them on muesli and orange juice. I couldn't help but see the irony; the working-man's bacon, eggs and fried bread had become both a kind of party treat and a symbol of first-class privilege.

I got quite accustomed to first class and, despite my rebellious streak, no one so much as raised an eyebrow until five years after the incident with Elaine, when I had another brush with a British Rail jobsworth. After buying a sandwich and a beer at the buffet, I turned to go back to my seat, only to find my way barred by an official arm.

'Second class is back that way, sir,' he said nastily.

'I am first class,' I spluttered. In no mood for games, I thrust my ticket at him straight away.

I wanted him to grovel, like the little fat bloke had, but he just shrugged and reluctantly let me pass. But I felt no sense of victory, not with a queue of standard-class passengers enjoying some free entertainment at my expense. That'll teach him to be a snob, they thought. They were on the side of the British Rail ape, not mine. I was so upset that when I got home I wrote to InterCity to complain. I still have their reply:

'I am sorry you feel we have a 'stereotype'
First-Class passenger in mind. We are happy to
see you travel in your denims and trainers, but
you obviously must recognise that this being the
exception, rather than the rule, people do tend to
question this.
   Our staff generally, I hope, do not take the
action that you outlined in your letter and
obviously we would be pleased to see you travel
with us, whether it be First Class or Standard
Class, and would not I hope make you feel
awkward because of your attire.'

I often wonder how many first-class passengers really enjoy their privilege. It doesn't take much to make them feel bashful or self-conscious, especially when some old dear totters through the carriage with her suitcase heading for the hot and overcrowded standard class. There's a flicker of biblical guilt, just for a moment, until the old lady is followed by a family from a council estate, with two chocolatey kids and a carrier bag of snacks. These are the people, gloriously blind to the class divide, who commandeer a table and start sharing out the Penguins. No one dare point out the family's mistake – do they want a knuckle sandwich? – so they look forward to the inevitable ejection and enjoy it with smug amusement. We love the discomfort of others at the best of times, but when it's all tied up with class, it becomes something particularly and distastefully British.

I've given up travelling first class now, except at weekends when it costs an extra fiver and is full of students and pensioners, the kind of people who deserve a taste of luxury now and then. Though with lasting memories of Yugoslavia, I wonder if they don't Shake 'n' Vac the carriages before returning them to their normal duties. How distressing it would be for a besuited sales rep to find an old lady's hairgrip sticking in his pants.

My foreign freebies were always first class, of course, but I was happily conscience-free about those. Apart from the last time I went to France with Jinx when, even with his concessions, he could only afford a second-class ticket (at least the French still have the honesty to call it first and second). What was I to do? It would have been daft for us to sit in separate carriages, but on the other hand I was reluctant to forgo the luxury of first-class travel as I sped from Paris to Avignon on the TGV. Talk about a moral dilemma.

In the end, socialism won the day and I sat in second class with Jinx, much to the bafflement of the ticket inspector. I know he asked me about it, and tried to explain that I was needlessly discomforting myself. Since it would have been hard to explain such a quirk in English, let alone in schoolboy French, I just smiled and let him do his Gallic shrug. But I can't help thinking that if the same thing had happened at home, some of those British Rail inspectors (sorry, Revenue Protection Officers) would have insisted I moved into first.

026   Almost Virtual Reality: The Severn Valley Railway, 1988

In the late eighties I suddenly 'acquired' a fourteen-year-old son. (The details are too emotionally coloured to belong in a book about trainspotting, but readers might put two and two together.) I didn't have a clue how to begin making amends for those fourteen years apart. W. H. Smith had a 'Parenting' section jam-packed with books full of breathing exercises for mums-to-be and advice for fussing fathers, but nothing for men like me who found themselves on the spot. Nor was there anyone I could turn to for advice. I had to fumble my way through it, clutching at the first thing I thought might help bond us. And, at all costs, I was determined to avoid visits to McDonald's or the zoo.

Our first outing as father and son was to the Railway Museum at York. The place was full of lovingly restored railway engines, every one as pretty as a carnival organ. But I felt uneasy as we walked from exhibit to exhibit on floors as quiet as a whisper, and not once did I hear the crack of a piece of coal underfoot. Though imaginatively housed in the old MPD, the greatest irony is that the museum is now a smoke-free zone; the slightest whiff would be enough to set off the state-of-the-art alarm system and have the punters stampeding for the exit. The walls were full of the old nameplates, but they might as well have been mass-produced horse brasses for all they had to do with real railways. It looked like trainspotting's trophy room, a display of all the nice bits, snapped off from real life, and thus quite meaningless. Everything here was too good to be true. It wasn't so much that Martin was bored (even children want to see the coach where Victoria did her widdle) but it was unlikely to fire him with enthusiasm. We visited the shop and returned home with the obligatory jigsaws and reproduction posters, but it hadn't been the triumph I'd been hoping for.

I didn't want Martin to see my past as a museum exhibit – a school cap and a biro and a bottle of pop artfully arranged in a glass display case – I wanted him to smell it for real, all the smoke and the sulphur and the sizzling grease. I wanted him to hear the rattle of wagons in the sidings and whistle at the flattened penny that was still warm to the touch. Then I'd just keep my fingers crossed in the hope that the fire would catch, that in the railways he might see some fun he and I could share together, and in some way make up for vanished time. An arrogant wish really. Why should a child be stamped by his father's past? Why did it have to be on my terms? If I was so keen to bond, why didn't I take up skateboarding?

Only twenty yards separates the BR station at Kidderminster from the terminus of the Severn Valley Railway, but it's quite easy to kid yourself you've slipped back forty years. The benches in the ticket hall are solidly wooden, polished by a hundred years of fidgeting bottoms. Up on the wall, poster girls beckon us to join them for fun on the beach. There's a little half-oval ticket window, small enough to preserve the mystery and ritual of the ticket clerk's job, and even the act of bending to it is a lot like being in a confessional; you can't see the man, only his chin and mouth, but you have to do business with him.

'One and a half return to Bewdley, please.'

Visually the station is a treat, but it snags the other senses too. The thump of the old ticket-dating machine could be an echo that has taken thirty years to return. Even the air smells old. Warmed by the sunlight the woodwork releases long-hidden aromas from the 1940s: lonely cigarettes, rain-damp mackintoshes, a twist of cologne. It can be quite spooky when the past engages all your senses simultaneously, but as you emerge from the booking hall and see a man selling Cornettos and hot dogs things ripple back to reality. It's quite a relief to get your bearings again.

A train of 'rhubarb and custard' coaches is already waiting for us at the long and uncrowded platform, its doors flung back, open and inviting. We have time to stand alongside the engine and give it the once-over, and I can't resist slipping into lecturer mode.

'Well, Martin, this is a "Manor" class 4–6–0 mixed traffic loco designed by Hawksworth and built at Swindon . . .'

Martin is interested in the loco and, so close to the heat and the pent-up pressure, instinctively respectful of its power. My commentary is irrelevant. Does it matter how many wheels the Manor has or who built it? He looks slightly betrayed by my sudden change of role, from dad to tour guide, and I have to make an effort to stop myself from waffling.

After all our 1968 end-of-steam agony things couldn't have worked out better. Britain is chock-a-block with preserved railways – The Great Central, The South Devon, The Severn Valley, The Keighley and Worth Valley, and a hundred others, so many of them that it seems we've created a parallel world, a country where time stopped around 1947. Most of the lines make a profit too, for which we should be grateful. Steam-age purists object to the gimmickry which brings in those profits – Thomas The Tank Weekends, Hot Cross Bun Specials, Santa's Express – but you can't blame the managers for exploring every angle if it keeps the line alive and viable. And the kids love it. Still, it must be a shock for an old spotter who turns up for communion with his favourite Castle, an old friend from the past, and sees a huge Thomas face smirking at him from the smokebox door. But no one has a monopoly on old railway engines, and if we can share the pleasure in different ways, all the better for their survival. In any case, these are one-off events. When the weekenders have returned home in their Escorts, the railways return to their most devoted admirers, those men who love them for their moods, not their eager-to-please grins.

The day is full of illusions. It's not just the steamers and old carriages that trick me. Sitting opposite Martin, I feel as if it's not just him who is fourteen, but me as well. We're back in 1965, two kids on a spotting trip. I've been making silly squeaking noises with the arm of the seat, and now, in the hope of amusing him, I bash the seat cushions with my fist, sending up mushroom clouds of ancient dust.

'Dad . . .' Martin looks embarrassed, in the panic-stricken way that only teenagers can, and looks to the door to make sure no one's passing by.

I should remember that I'm a father now as well as an adult. But today is proving especially difficult. This is my *Blue Remembered Hills* time and the realization that I can't return to 1965 is quite depressing.

There are one or two spectators standing about on Arley station, and I deliberately avoid the use of the

Timeless. A prairie tank runs 'tender first' out of Bridgnorth on the Severn Valley Railway. 1958 or 1988?

T-word here. We're not amongst trainspotters at the Severn Valley. There is nothing to spot, as such, and none of these men has come in the hope of copping anything new. They've all seen 7812 and 43106 and 45110 a dozen times before. The enthusiasts here today are a different kind of spotter. With their camcorders and

Pentaxes they seek to capture something more elusive than mere numbers – gauzy, floating mirages of their own childhoods, perhaps, moments glimpsed through a gap in the steam. But, in a disappointing reversal of the cliché, when the film is developed the smudge that looks like a 1950s schoolboy has vanished. It is a paradox, this use of technology in such a spiritual pursuit, and I can't help thinking a Ouija board would be more appropriate. The best thing about this place is that it's all pain-free and we've got all the time in the world to enjoy it. On the Severn Valley there are no withdrawals, no neglect, no scrappings. These Manors, Halls and Blackies are as close to eternal as can be. This is locomotive heaven.

We've been eminently successful in recreating semi-rural England. These stations have been lovingly restored with gas lights and Great Western firebuckets, Gold Flake advertisements and penny chocolate machines. A door creaks open at the end of the platform and out steps an old-fashioned railwayman. He looks at the departing train, plucks a watch out his waistcoat pocket, and nods with evident satisfaction. But these aren't real staff, they're trainspotters in disguise, men who get their thrills for free by giving up their weekends to play at signalmen, stationmasters and porters. No role is too menial for them. It's not just the uniform that looks convincing, this chap has even got the unconcerned amble off to a T.

The surprising thing is that these volunteers are not all oldies who remember the steam age. This railwayman looks as if he would be more at home at a Dire Straits concert. Yet there's no denying his enthusiasm and commitment; he's even grown mutton-chop whiskers to fit in with the period flavour. On the other hand he may have bought them from a joke shop.

This *trompe-l'oeil* doesn't always work. The thing is, the steam locos and the cute little stations aren't all we miss. It's the whole thing, a scale of operations that even the most dedicated enthusiasts could never recreate: the round-the-clock railway scene, the sepulchral gloom of the sheds, the clang of buffers in the goods yard, the ghostly whistle in the small hours, the night train throwing panicked shadows against the slummy houses.

There are half a dozen engines on shed at Bewdley, enough to make it look busy, and with clinker crunching underfoot and oily puddles for the unwary to ruin their Hush Puppies in, the place looks much like one of the smaller depots I might have bunked in the sixties. I take a few snaps of Martin, sitting on an old boiler, standing on the footplate of a Blackie. No one bothers us, and that's part of the trouble. I wish we weren't welcome, I wish I could share with Martin the adrenalin thrill of bunking a shed. Wouldn't it be a perfect bonding thing for us if some old codger of a foreman was to come out of his office and chase us off?

Steam fans are chasing a past which is always receding. To stop it dwindling like the dot on a telly screen they've had to resort to rewriting history. Not once, but every decade or so. Gresley's A3 *Flying Scotsman*, for instance, was originally preserved as LNER loco 4472 and painted apple green. But the spotters who remember that look are dead, or senile, so to please the kids from the fifties, the ones with the spending power and who want value for money, it has been repainted and reidentified with its British Railways number 60103. The old guard hate it – where has their apple-green beauty gone? – but as they die off so do their opinions and values. And so it goes on. How deep is our affection, then, at the end of the day? When *Flying Scotsman* was in its 1940s guise it did nothing for me. I yawned every time I saw it. But now it has its sixties look I can willingly join in with loving it.

Having *Flying Scotsman* preserved ought to be enough, but it isn't. Everyone wants their 'rights' these days. What about the old spotters who wanted to see another A3, *Brown Fox*, say, which was dragged off to the scrapyard well before the preservation bandwagon got going?

Tough. They just had to lump it. Until someone asked why should they? The railway was theirs, and so were the engines, they could do anything they liked. Such as have two fibre-glass *Brown Fox* nameplates made, paint 60036 on the cabside, and, hey presto!, who'd know the difference?

No one can be sure what is real any more. The railways have invented their own version of virtual reality in the belief that everything can be recreated. Nighttime events; so that photographers can recapture that special nocturnal atmosphere. Mock freights; trainloads of empty wagons on a pointless journey, going nowhere, delivering nothing. Train numbers aren't important any more. Everything is done for the benefit of the assembled photographers. It all makes me very uneasy. Nostalgia is mainly harmless, but cut loose from its ethereal plane and harnessed to trickery, who knows where it will end?

Did it work? I ask myself at the end of the day, as Martin and I head back to Burton on our bog unit. Did the smell of steam and the clatter of an old-fashioned railway impress him? I'm not sure. It's been a less hushed experience than York, more tactile, more crunchy all round. It would be such a thrill for me if Martin took the heavy hint and became a trainspotter, but I know it's a hopeless wish. This toytown steam railway, however lovingly recreated, is just another theme park.

Martin isn't saying anything. He's borrowed my Walkman and is solemnly appraising the *Sergeant Pepper* cassette. He seems to like it, and maybe I should be content with that small cross-generation victory.

British steam buffs had a nasty shock in 1993. The Eurocrats in Brussels noticed them. All these years they'd been happily throwing coal about, stoking up fires, letting off high-pressure steam; the whole business was as old-fashioned and as wacky as an *It's A Knockout* game. But the nannyish rule-makers were concerned about all the hot surfaces and scalding steam. Not withstanding the fact that many of the drivers were old hands and accepted burns and scalds as an occupational hazard, Brussels decided that they needed protection. In future all hot surfaces had to be clearly flagged with fluorescent yellow stripes and warning signs in four languages. And that would apply as much to Castles and Blackies as it would to the school boiler and the oven in the local caff. When the steam buffs realized that their beloved engines, so painstakingly restored in liveries of apple green and crimson lake, would have to be painted fluorescent yellow, they were horrified. The future suddenly became hideous.

In the end, Britain managed to get itself a waiver, as it so often does. It was a victory for common sense, but there were distinct overtones of old-fashioned patriotism. We'd stopped them messing about with our sausages and by jingo did they really think we'd let 'em paint our lovely steamers like dayglo zebras?

Today's Scene

027 A Day at the Speedway

Lichfield's Trent Valley station has always been a favourite destination. As teenagers with bikes we could be there in half an hour, a straight run down the A38, with the slipstreams of speeding lorries to help us along. A great dodge for a summer-holiday day and, best of all, it cost us nothing.

To kids from Burton, where trains were dependable plodders for the most part, the Trent Valley line was decidedly exotic, a silver speedway through the flat Midlands scenery. The Euston and Liverpool expresses were no longer hauled by Coronations or Scots, but it was still a thrill to watch the blue electrics burning round the tilted curve at 80-odd m.p.h. Attention was vital; sometimes they flashed by so quickly you could miss the number completely. Nothing ever went this fast through Burton.

Few trains deigned to stop, and the daily routine left plenty of spare time for staff to cultivate flowerbeds and construct a rockery in which LICHFIELD TRENT VALLEY was spelt out with big butter-coloured stones. The countrified ambiance was spoilt only by the pinched whistle of the expresses and the tangle of overhead wires which fizzed with trapped energy. In the afternoons, though, a couple of stopping trains would slide out of the heat haze and set off a brief flurry of activity. A door creaked open and a porter came blinking into the light, parcel sacks were thrown on and off, the station master cracked a joke with the driver, and very occasionally a passenger boarded or alighted.

Trent Valley had no buffet, nothing at all to sustain trainspotters apart from a solitary chocolate machine with a choice of Cadbury's Dairy Milk or the ubiquitous Payne's Poppets. There was a pub, though, at the end of the station drive, and one of us would be deputized

Sixties classic. One of the first-generation electrics
whizzing through Lichfield T.V. in the mid-sixties

to pedal up and buy a bottle of limeade and four packets
of cheesy biscuits from the off sales.

So much for the memories. It's always a danger to
return to these places which once meant so much, but a
trainspotter with any kind of track record just can't avoid
it.

Until recently Trent Valley station was a dignified
building of red brick, with fretworked awnings that
offered shelter from the rain, and deep grey shade from
the sun. All that's gone now, replaced by a prefabricated
ticket office and, on the up platform, a glorified bus shelter with squeaky tip-up seats. Time was when the British
waited for their trains with a mixture of impatience and
resigned languor. It was done in style and privacy. Now
even that has been trivialized. I suspect that the architects (does a bus shelter need an architect?) want us to
look like the model citizens on their sketches – pretty
and stylish and completely fictional. Law-abiding as I

am, I can't help but feel some sympathy for whoever has scrawled 'Baz and Sue were here' in felt-tip on the glass. It may be unsightly, but as a protest against such sterility it can scarcely be called vandalism. In much the same way, I'm grateful for the presence of trainspotters. They are totally superfluous individuals, neither staff nor passengers, devoid of any function except to muck up the nice vistas of marketing departments and architects. They remind me of those smirking faces that always manage to get in the background when an MP or company spokesperson is being interviewed on TV, deflating any attempt at subterfuge.

Apart from the expresses, flung northwards on a cat's cradle of wires, time still ticks slowly at Trent Valley. Maybe that is part of its continued attraction. Trainspotting has, for many adherents, a purely meditative function. While some people sit by gurgling streams or on top of hills, there are contemplative figures who prefer to do their gazing alongside railway lines. They're not collecting numbers, they don't take photographs, nor do they even display much emotion when an express cracks through the station. A bench on a deserted platform is their retreat from the hurly-burly. What better idyll on a summer Saturday in England? Birds twitter, spiders build webs between the broken bricks, and in the short siding that was already disused in 1966, the rails rust with painful and infinite slowness.

Appreciating all this, I do feel a bit guilty for introducing two boisterous children into the scene. You can't expect children to appreciate the meditative function of railways, as for them it's pure magic. Despite all the blandishments of the car culture, it has nothing that even comes close to the singing thrill and the fearsome unleashed heaviness of a Class 90 cracking along at 100 m.p.h. The squeaky-clean bodywork of modern cars is quite alien to children. Grime and grinding is what grabs them, so what better than to watch a growling 56 stickied up with an honest patina of grease and brake dust?

It gives me a queer turn sometimes, returning to these old haunts. Apart from drastic changes to the station, Lichfield TV is much the same as I've always remembered it. Summer-holiday weather, the dusty fragrance of grass, blue skies with the needle glint of an aeroplane bound for the Americas, and the shimmering heat haze down the line, out of which the trains would slide, the speed distorted by the perspective until they were right on top of you, then an elongated blur of windows and paintwork and faces. Standing here on the station, changed as it is, I can see myself perched on the wall of the sidings, leaning down and backwards to my saddlebag to grab my spotting book or a bag of crisps. I can almost remember snatches of conversation. Then I blink and cough to wake myself – and I'm standing here with two children of my own. It's *Twilight Zone* stuff, creepy and inexplicable and yet possessing an internal logic of its own.

The afternoon-stopping trains are still going. But the greatest surprise is that one of them (017) is so anti-quated that it was probably doing the same job back in 1966 when we V-signed it out of the way because it was blocking our view of the fast line.

As well as the main Euston–Crewe line, Trent Valley also boasts a 'high level'. In the heyday of the railways dozens of towns had more than one station, and there were several where one line crossed over or under another: Tamworth, Wigan, Retford, and at Newark two main lines cross each other on the same level. At Lich-field, two very different cultures crossed each other at right angles; the clean and speedy InterCity future whizzing through below, while up above steam-hauled freights still plodded their way to Derby or Dudley.

Lichfield's High Level station was shut to passengers in the sixties and left to rot slowly under a thin slime of moss. The line has recently been reopened to passengers (as have several others around the country in council-led initiatives) and platforms here are now the northern terminus of the West Midlands' Cross-City Link. Maybe it doesn't have the bustle it used to have, but it's good to see life again after years of neglect.

They don't call it Trent Valley High Level any more, though. Such old-fashioned concepts are a real bugbear for today's PR department. And I suppose it must have been a mouthful at the ticket office: 'Child Day Return to Lichfield Trent Valley High Level, please.' It's a shame, however. All these arcane definitions added considerably to the mystique and variety of railway life. What price now Hull Paragon, Templecombe Upper, Carlisle Citadel, or those dozens of Victorias and Exchanges? The railway management reluctantly hold on to Bristol Temple Meads and Exeter St David's, if only to distinguish them from other stations in the same town, but given half a chance their history and poetry would be consigned to the bin. But those distinctive names are embedded in me for always, even the ones that have been quietly dropped, and I often try to catch the ticket office out by asking for a return to Wolverhampton High Level, Derby Midland or Cheltenham Spa Landsdowne.

Trent Valley station may have changed, but the signal box hasn't. It looked old-fashioned even in the sixties, a steam-age structure marooned between the speeding electric trains. The windows down at track level were already blackened by years of smoke and dirty water, and they've never been cleaned since. Windolene would be no use now, you'd probably need a paintscraper and a gallon of vinegar.

Remembering the military smartness of the erstwhile stationmaster – polished shoes, peaked cap, clipped moustache – it's a shock to realize that the signalman high up in his eyrie has a ponytail.

I must confess that I've always been quietly envious of the signalman's job. I've often imagined myself having a cushy number on some lonely freight branch, with little to do except lean on the verandah smoking a calm cigarette on a summer's day, and in winter sit beside a coal stove tapping out a bestseller on a portable typewriter. Though no doubt signal operators will tell me I'm harbouring foolish dreams.

This line was the focus of some notoriety a few years back after a suspiciously large number of people fell out of speeding trains. Newspapers dubbed it the 'Tamworth Triangle'. All manner of explanations were offered. The passengers were drunk, fooling about, said British Rail. The railways are falling apart, said the public. Either way, I'm glad I wasn't on the station at the time, judging by the gruesome tales I heard. Like old sailors, railwaymen love spinning yarns, and the more horrible the better.

Still, it was a peculiar affair. I even harboured a crackpot theory about an evil presence haunting the line (as well as these incidents, there've been a lot of crashes and deaths along here: at Lichfield in 1946, Nuneaton in 1975, and the biggest one, Harrow in 1952). I could picture, like a scene in a film, the door locks supernaturally sliding open while an unwitting passenger leans at the window to enjoy the scenery. It made me think, with a retrospective shiver of danger, of all those years I spent leaning on the doors. But it never occurred to me that they could be unsafe. I had an unquestioning faith in the skills and the maintenance of the men at the carriage works.

028   A Postcard From Dawlish

I've been here before, I thought, when I pitched up at Dawlish on my first Western railrover in 1968. Actually, until then, I'd never been further west than Bristol, but I recognized Dawlish instantly. I'd seen it a thousand times on holiday postcards, jigsaws, toffee-tin lids and on the covers of old annuals bought at jumble sales. The picture of a Great Western Castle at the head of a holiday

Sun, sea, sky and steam. *Manorbier Castle* drifts alongside
the beach at Teignmouth

train skirting the sea wall, puffing cutesy cottonwool
smoke over the heads of the holidaymakers, is one of the
enduring icons from the Golden Age. It still turns up
even now, especially, I've noticed, on birthday cards for
men in the 45–60 age group.

I'd missed the Castles and Kings by a good five years
in 1968, but didn't I have those quirky little Warships and
the magnificent Westerns instead? Where else on British
Rail did you get hydraulics? And where else did they have
maroon livery and cast numberplates on diesels?

Back at school I'd got some photographs as proof I'd
been to Dawlish, but they were poor evidence of the real
glories of the place. In black and white how could I really
convince anyone about the terracotta red of the cliffs and
the maroonness of the hydraulics? They wouldn't even
believe it when I told them there were palm trees growing
close to Dawlish station.

This holiday line, from Paddington to the West Country, is where trainspotting started. The Great Western, PR-wise before the term had even been invented, milked their holidaymakers for every penny. Gimmicks and souvenirs abounded: GWR teatowels, GWR crockery, GWR guidebooks. To keep children amused on long journeys there were games and jigsaws. And lists of Great Western locos to look out for along the way. Simple self-promotion it may have been, but they'd hit on a winner. The lists soon became the latest craze and rival railway companies quickly copied the idea. In 1942 the first Ian Allan *ABC*s were issued and the whole trainspotting thing took off.

Some people have never heard of Dawlish, yet, trainspotters or not, they'd know it straight away. The image of the trains skirting the sea is filed away in the folk memory, part of our collective watercolour dream of old-fashioned Britain. Steam trains, seaside, children waving; it's got all the right ingredients. Even the newly privatized rail companies still use it on their pamphlets, knowing quite well that when it comes to winning hearts and minds the best brains in marketing will never think up a more appealing image.

The line needn't have been constructed along the coast like this, but Isambard Kingdom Brunel was a showman and a maverick who wanted something impressive. It certainly was that, but I.K. left British Rail with an awful headache in track maintenance work. In the winter the waves can rear up from the sea, smashing against the station walls, washing across the tracks where the ballast, so easily worried away, has to be securely tied with steel netting. Dawlish is impressive for being the only bit of British Rail to have a station perched above the promenade in such a daring and appealing way. What other station could set you down so directly in the heart of holidayland? From up on the cliffs it looks fragile and precariously poised, but closer inspection shows it to be solid, built to sound

Victorian values with stiff girders and bolts as big as walnuts.

Even now, in the age of the car, on a summer Saturday the trains still come through Dawlish every ten minutes. During the thirties and after the war it must have been an amazing procession.

Dawlish has always been good cinema too, and I've got the videos. I've watched *The Ghost Train* countless times, but the anarchic humour is still fresh every viewing. Arthur Askey pulls the communication cord as the train passes Dawlish, then goes chasing his 'titfer' along the track while the loco simmers and the guard goes mad. In a later film, not quite equal to the classic status of *The Ghost Train*, neighbouring Teignmouth was renamed Tinmouth when Norman Wisdom went there to botch up the world of journalism.

They weren't the only jokers who visited. In 1969 I persuaded Jinx to accompany me on a Western railrover. Our favourite prank was to lean out of the train and strafe the strolling holidaymakers with peashooters. Harmless schoolboy fun, but I often feel guilty about it, as if I betrayed that very thing which makes Dawlish special. We didn't do it that often, though. Once, a train stopped unexpectedly, and one of our victims, a man with tattoos, sprinted towards the station bent on punishment. He didn't quite make it, but it was scary enough to put us on our best behaviour from then on.

And you don't have to be a trainspotter to find Dawlish thrilling. This is where trains touch the rest of the population, where the kids who've come 300 miles on the motorway, trussed into their seats like turkeys, begin to wonder if they've been missing out. InterCity 125s may not be ideal images for toffee-tin lids, but the thrill's still there. Children still look up from their sandcastles every time a train passes (unless it's a Sprinter) and the passengers – old ladies, backpackers, even businessmen – still wave back to the paddlers and deckchair loungers and wish they could join in the fun. At times like these, relaxed, inspired, you can't help but think of the emotional poverty of the car culture, the joyful communism of the trains versus the puritan hypocrisy of the automobile.

But there are dark forces at work. Motoring and airline values continue to seep into the railways, destroying their charm. Passengers are sealed in now, air-conditioned and sound-insulated, but they press close against the windows and look longingly out. Marketing people try so hard to impress travellers with comfort, but they deny them the simple pleasures. What these passengers really want to do is fling open the windows and lean out for a lungful of salty seaside air.

There's no doubting that I had an emotional attachment to Dawlish, a love that was mixed up with the railways, but which was so much more as well. It was around 1969 that I first began to suspect that there was something more to trainspotting than simply amassing a book full of numbers. Half of it was about the trains, sure enough, but the other half was about something much more universal. Sitting up on Langstone Rock with Jinx during the 1970 rover, I was overcome by emotion, humming Beethoven's 'Song of Joy' (there was a pop version in the charts just then) as the trains headed along the coast. But emotion is not quite the ticket on a trainspotting jaunt, so I knew I'd have to keep it private.

Between 1976 and 1990 I never went to Dawlish at all, though I often thought of it and sometimes a maroon shadow slid through my dreams, gone when I awoke, leaving me angry for not catching the number. The nearest I came was when I went for a job as a copywriter at a tiny advertising agency in Exmouth. It was a desperate move and, since none of the posh London agencies seemed to want me, I knew I'd have to leave an otherwise enjoyable London life behind. Still, if I felt lonely I'd always have had the railways, and it would have been

The Year of Privatization: a glorified 'bog unit' skirts
the sea wall at Dawlish in 1994

only a five-minute ferry ride across the Exe to Dawlish.

Though the steamers have long gone, and even the Warships and Westerns are a seventies memory, the trainspotters still come here. For some of them it's just a couple of hours, a stopover between the serious spotting at Plymouth and Exeter. But others stay longer, booking into one of the bed and breakfasts that cash in on their lineside location with adverts in the railway magazines. Jinx often organizes the family holiday here, so he can watch trains while his wife and children lick 99s and play pitch 'n' putt. He thinks he's being smart, but I suspect his wife cottoned on to his dodge years ago.

But maybe spotters aren't coming as often as they used to. The last locos to haul trains here regularly were the Hoovers, but they've gone now. There have been enough enthusiasts over the years for Dawlish to have had its own railway bookshop, run by an enthusiast. It's a sign of the times that the premises are now deserted, though in its windows the pictures and the book covers linger defiantly to remind townspeople and visitors of the glories of Dawlish.

At midnight Dawlish is as quiet as the grave. The pubs and the chip shop are shut, Belisha beacons blink unregarded and the only sound comes from the slap of waves against the breakwater. The station is lit up, but totally deserted. Except for one loner with a flask and a pair of binoculars. The police would probably take him for a burglar, a passer-by for some kind of voyeur, but watching from my holiday flat, I know he's just a trainspotter. At this time of day there are no holiday trains to record, no friendly railwayman to chat to, just solitude and discomfort. What on earth can be the attraction? Then a Railfreight 37 with half a dozen tanker wagons emerges from the tunnel and rattles up the coastline. It's at times like this you know trainspotting is worthwhile.

029   Notes From an Open Day: Worcester, 1994

From the old Derby Works Flower Show right up to the Severn Valley's Diesel Gala Weekends, railway open days are part of a long tradition. I love the atmosphere; broadened out from mere trainspotting, leavened with a colourful crowd of wives and children, it's as quaintly English as a village fête. There's no Miss Marple, of course, but there are bound to be a few clergymen wandering around the old goods yard behind Shrub Hill station.

Children, as well as vicars, also love trains, and parents love an excuse to bring them along. They start them young, before they can even hold a biro; everywhere you look there are pushchairs juddering across the ballast or being lifted up across the rails as Dad homes in on a favourite engine. At Worcester the locos are all static, so there's no danger and older kids can wander at will. The Yorky ice-cream van is doing a roaring trade in 99s.

This isn't trainspotting as such, since no one expects to see anything fresh or out of the ordinary, it's more of an event in the trainspotting season. You just have to show your face, that's the main thing. No one wants to be left without a point of view when the subject of Worcester comes up over a pint, even if it's only along the lines of: 'Worcester? Bloody Sprinter was diverted via Lichfield because of engineering. We were forty minutes late getting in.'

One of the big attractions of an open day is the chance to climb up in the loco cabs and pull a few levers. Hauling myself up the steps into the cab of E3003 (one of the old blue-painted electrics that used to bowl along the Trent Valley line at 90 m.p.h.) I bump into my first clergyman. He's semi-disguised in trainers and jeans, but his tweedy jacket and dog-collar are a dead give away. Perched in the driver's seat, he presses all the buttons like an excited child and whistles high-speed fantasies through his teeth.

The festival atmosphere is coloured by the sound of Dire Straits over the loudspeakers. Spotter-mockers joke about sad men in anoraks listening to old Kathy Kirby records or folky singalongs about navvies blasting their way through the Pennines, but pop music has always been important for rail fans. In the heyday of British pop, groups wrote about railways without any self-consciousness. The Beatles had 'Ticket to Ride' and 'Day Tripper', of course, but there were all kinds of oblique references elsewhere, in the Kinks' 'Waterloo Sunset', where Terry met Julie at Waterloo Station; Paul Simon's 'Homeward Bound', 'sitting on the railway station with a ticket to my destination'; and the Seekers with their lovely 'train whistle blowing, makes a sleepy noise'.

Privatization has already reared its ugly head at Worcester. Some of the promised exhibits have failed to turn up. Under the new rules, anyone who owns a locomotive has to pay Railtrack for the privilege of travelling over their rails. It's an extra cost that's too much for some of the preservation groups. Hence there's no Warship or Class 52, which is a great disappointment to many visitors, including me. But their owners have managed to bring themselves, if not their precious locos, and have set up a stand from where they can rattle their collecting tins and sell souvenir booklets.

The ragged parade of stalls alongside the tracks is doing good business. Or rather, it attracts lots of interest. I don't know how many of the browsers actually part with any cash. The stallholders aren't here to provide a free show, but they watch good-naturedly while a motley procession of bashers flick through old timetables and rule books, or ponder whether a *Mallard* eraser is a good buy at 30p.

At the serious end of the collecting business, a stout

chequebook is essential. It's hard to believe how the prices of relics have inflated. A numberplate from a steam loco – probably nicked in the first place – will now set you back at least £100, or up to £500 if it's from a Castle or a Jubilee. (If you haven't got the money, don't worry. You can buy a realistic resin one for £9.50.) Even an uninspiring metal sign from Carshalton station circa 1966 has a price tag of £150 stickered to it. Wandering up and down I keep an eye out for my Horninglow name-plate, though I don't know what I'd do if I saw it.

What fascinates me most is the bric-a-brac, particu-larly a set of buttons from a stationmaster's uniform. But what do you actually do with them? Sew them on your favourite cardigan, or keep them in a special button-collector's album? There are knives and forks from the old Great Western, looking seriously tarnished, but imbued with nostalgia. But you couldn't set out this cutlery for your guests without making them wonder about your mental state. Perhaps it's a solitary pleasure. You eat your fish fingers and Bird's-Eye peas with them and, half-closing your eyes, imagine yourself in the restaurant car of the Cheltenham Flyer one summer's evening back in 1957.

At least there's something old-fashioned about the GWR cutlery. But who on earth would want a British Rail teapot from the 1970s? What fond memories could it possibly hold, apart from a buffet car full of Brummie businessmen with kipper ties? No, not even for £3, I'm sorry. And anyway, the lid doesn't close properly.

I haven't seen many anoraks today. Everything but: tracksuits, camouflage jackets, baseball caps, tweedy M&S jackets. There are one or two anoraks, but no more than in an average cross-section of British society. Who cares what people are wearing anyway? One of the best things about trainspotting is that you don't need to dress up. There's no pose involved. It's the unaffected and democratic principles of childhood that count here. No one gives a stuff what you're dressed in. We're here to have fun and not bitch about each other's togs.

St Paddy (back with its old pre-TOPS number of D9001) is one of the star exhibits. It's one of those gods of the wind that bellowed 'get out of my goddamned way!' as it cracked through Grantham. Now, high up in the cab, it's amazing to be reminded how old-fashioned these early diesels were. The brake levers and gears are as chunky as they were in the steam age. Even the buttons and dials, which were certainly hi-tech in their day, look clumsy and primitive to our modern eyes. But then it's all too easy to mock old technology from the recent past.

Worcester is crawling with photographers. And it's not only the trains that are captured for posterity; there are so many cameras clicking and camcorders whirring that you can't help but get in someone's way. I find it queer to think that some time in the future, next week or next year, a group of train buffs gathered in a front room with the curtains drawn will hiss tetchily as you stumble across the creatively framed view of Hoover 50027 and yell, just as the photographer did, 'Get out the way, you prat!'

There's one way to get round the problem. At Exeter, three weeks previously, they held a special day just for photographers. And charged them £8 for the privilege. But since every serious spotter has a camera these days, and hundreds of them turned up at Exeter, I can't really see how it cures the problem of people wandering across your viewfinder.

For half the afternoon I've been chasing up and down the yard, jumping up in the air as I try to see over the roofs of carriages. I keep insisting that there's a steam engine here, though there was no mention of one in the programme. 'I can hear it, listen!' I shout. Robin and Mark trail patiently after me, until I realize I've been pursuing a mirage – it's the sounds from a steam-age LP that one of the stallholders has been playing over his loudspeakers. I feel a right berk! Now that those old recordings have been remastered and stuck on a CD, a steam buff can scarcely tell the difference.

There's always been a market for sound recordings of trains, steam and diesel. Quality varies. I had *Sounds of the Great Western* crisply defined on an Argo Transacord LP, but *Shunting in the Yard* is a mish-mash of hissing and clanging, some of it recorded in a downpour. It shows admirable dedication by the train enthusiast (or did he just stick his mike out the window?) but on a hissy cassette, the sound of pouring rain is virtually indistinguishable from billowing steam. The only joy I get from *Shunting in the Yard* is turning it up full blast and watching man next door scratch his head when he hears the whistle of a Jinty and the clang of wagon buffers.

On the train home I have that lovely end-of-the-day feeling I used to get years ago, a glorious fatigue, lullabied by the rhythm of the wheels and the sway as we rock across the points. You're out in the wild world, no more safe than a pea rattling in a cocoa tin, but this is your milieu and you know no possible harm can come to you. When I get home I'll sleep the sleep of the just.

The next day there's always some paperwork to catch up with. I've bought a few souvenirs, but nothing that needs wall-brackets or regular oiling. One is an old *ABC* book. I say old, but though the staples are rusty it's never seen active service in a spotter's pocket. In that sense it lacks the true smell of history. With an *ABC* that's been knocked about a bit there's always a *frisson*, a sense of holding something that was once a vital part of some lad's spotting kit. But I'm often disapproving too; fancy underlining without using a ruler!, and how could they have bunked all the sub-sheds of Inverness when they lived in Dorset? Sometimes there's a name and address scrawled on the inside cover and I can't help wondering where the owner might be now. David Bailey of Whaley Bridge, for instance, whose 1959 Midland book has ended up in my possession, did you know that by the swinging sixties your ordinary name would be world famous?

My other souvenir of Worcester is a cabbing certificate. It cost 20p and proves that I've been up on the footplate of Class 40, D212. I know the owners have to make money somehow, but I was reluctant to fork out for this skinny bit of paper. Unless we were suspected of fudgery, our word was always our bond and we needed no certificates. We'd already cabbed half a dozen locos anyway, but I went up because Robin had heard the other kids sounding the klaxon and he wanted a go. The man who signed our certificates was apologetic, but so many people had already had a go that the train's hydraulics were fagged out and there was no hoot left in the pipes. I felt sorry for Robin. A cabbing certificate was no substitute for some hands-on fun and, I must confess, I quite fancied a blast myself.

030   Indoor Trainspotting: Derby, 1995

Derby was the first place I was allowed to go on my own. It was 1964. A Jubilee shunted empty newspaper wagons as we pulled into the station – 45611 *Hong Kong* (and I didn't need to look that up; my brain is full of mental snapshots whose colours have scarcely faded). Three decades later, and the Jubilees have long gone, of course, as have the faithful Peaks and cheerful Bo-Bos. Yet the spotters keep coming, quite happy, it seems, with the Sprinters and HSTs which have a virtual monopoly on passenger traffic. Trainspotters have been fighting this war of attrition for forty years now: will nothing ever make them pack up and go away? I suspect it's some kind of residual loyalty, a folk memory of when Derby was the epicentre of the Midland Railway, and its workshops rang with the sound of hammers, rather than lying virtually empty, as they do today.

Even this bleak January day with winds like Freddie Kreuger's fingernails isn't enough to put them off. But

I understand that too. Some of my fondest memories were of brass-monkey days. In common with most male hobbies (fishing, football, motorbike scrambling) trainspotting entails – no, demands – a reckless disregard for namby-pamby comforts like good weather. There's no need to overdo it, though, which is why some of them, including me, have retreated to the warmth of the station buffet. Through the window there's a clear view across Derby's six platforms, minimizing the risk of missing anything.

Sitting here with my 90p pot of tea and £1.47 sandwich, I can't help wondering how much the railways have made out of trainspotters over the years. Combined sales of sandwiches and tea and gooey fruit pies must have totted up a few million for a start. Add to that all those platform tickets intended as a miserly levy on people who simply wanted to see off their friends, but bought by trainspotters, and however much British Rail grumbled about kids larking about on stations spotters

Standardized nineties: An InterCity 125 at Derby in 1995

must have brought in enough over the years to pay for several Deltics. How long will it be, I wonder, before some whizz-kid accountant figures out the new railway companies are missing out? Trainspotters are loaded, he'll reason, why should they get all that pleasure from us for free? And I'm fairly certain that, after some initial protest, trainspotters would willingly pay 10p for entry to the platform.

Cheap and cheerful is a good description of a day at Derby, or Crewe or Grantham, and a vital clue to understanding some of the mockery. Since the public was trained to look on leisure as a product, and a product that must be paid for, they are unwilling to believe that fun can be had simply, and cheaply. There has to be a catch. And there is: being laughed at.

It was to Derby I came when, in 1993, I had to write a piece for the *Sunday Times* in support of trainspotters. Though they ought to have known better, the *Sunday Times*' Culture section was going to hunt with the media pack and run a clichéd portrait of a hobbyist with anorak, specs and multicoloured biros. A classic demolition job, in short. But at least they were going to play fair and run a defensive piece alongside it. I was overjoyed to get a commission from such a respected paper, but felt weighed with the burden. How could I possibly put the case for the defence in a mere 800 words?

The piece appeared, complete with front page picture of a nerd in specs, and the stink went up like a mushroom cloud. For weeks afterwards the railway magazines were full of letters from 'Disgusted of Doncaster' and 'Enraged of Enfield'. Quite apart from the fact that not one of them offered me any thanks for supporting them, or even seemed to have noticed my piece, I hated the way they rose to the bait, protesting about the multi-faceted aspects of the hobby (renovating old steamers, timing runs, making models, taking photographs) and redefining themselves as 'rail fans' or 'railway enthusiasts' or 'traction heritage preservationists'. In trying so hard to justify themselves they just dug themselves in deeper and looked more desperate. Despite their protests they had already accepted themselves as victims, thereby feeding a self-perpetuating prejudice.

Still, a lot of mockery might be deflected if trainspotting became tongue-in-cheek, as it used to be. Old nicknames (Jinties and Duck Sixes and Blackies, Tats and Bo-Bos and Baby Brushes) revealed humour and a healthy irreverence. But today DMUs are no longer called bog units, for instance, but are obediently referred

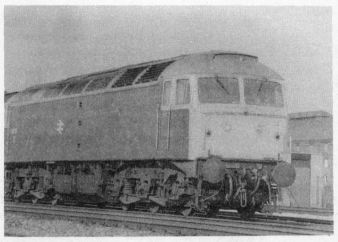

A Brush – sorry, Class 47 – on a passenger train in the mid-eighties

to by the official names thought up by marketing men: Sprinter, Pacer, etc. Some time in the eighties railway jargon got married to PR-speak, throwing up a whole load of gobbledegook which has been swallowed wholesale by many trainspotters. If railway management decides to rename a goods train a 'freight consist' magazines like *RAIL* adopt the term without a murmur of protest. Even the old guard are not immune. Their steam-hauled specials are no longer 'steam-hauled specials' but 'land cruises' with 'heritage traction'. Trainspotting has lost its sardonic edge, its ability to question such nonsense. Without that seed of irreverence at its heart it *is* a boring and laughable pastime. We were, and should be, at the lineside as observers, not as courtiers bowing and scraping.

Train magazines have come a long way since I used to buy *Railway World* in the sixties, but even if the language has lightened up, there's still too much deference, exemplified by this eagerness to recycle railway jargon. There is humour, of course there is, but in railway mags it seems that every pun and howler has to be signalled by several exclamation marks. All the mags do it, and it seems to have become endemic. The impression given is that no witticism must escape the reader's attention, no remarkable fact pass without a fanfare. I always feel as if I've been buttonholed by the pub bore, and the exclamation marks are the written equivalent of his over-familiar pokes on the shoulder.

Out on the platform again, with a take-away tea to warm the hands, a southbound train pulls in and a dishevelled head pokes out.

'Oi! Les.' He gives a wave to one of the spotters on the platform and, devilishly, leaps off before the train stops properly. Before joining Les, he looks at his reflection in the window of the waiting room and desperately tries to comb his hair back into shape. He's had his head out of the window most of the way from Sheffield. (It's no way to treat your hair, but it does blow away the dandruff.)

'Just bashed two class 90s on the East Coast,' he crows to Les. They're obviously old friends. 'Five late out of Doncaster, four early into Grantham. *Beast!*'

Les nods approvingly. Equipped with stopwatch and dog-eared timetable, Rog is one of trainspotting's time & motion men. Nothing moves on British Rail without them having a record of it. Their archives are monuments of trivia. If you want to know how fast the 16.10 Paignton–Leeds travelled on 5 June 1983, someone somewhere will be able to tell you. Millions of car journeys are made each day, each one forgotten as soon as the central-locking device clicks into place. Train movements, though, are faithfully logged and archived. Fast runs were great in the steam days, but even in the days of diesels and electrics, the feat's essentially the same, the teamwork of man and machine against a merciless clock and a supervisor out to kick your pants.

It sounds like a classic waste of time, yet Man has always been a diarist, a recording animal, a collector of statistics, and there has to be a reason. I like to think that one day, a hundred years in the future, it will be vital to know that the 16.24 Derby–Birmingham Sprinter was halted by a signal outside Wilnecote station and that the delay was exactly 88 seconds. These trainspotters with stopwatches have a vital mission, the relevance of which escapes us now, but for which future generations may well have cause to thank them.

Derby is a good place to be baffled. Timetable-phobia has been eliminated here: look even slightly bemused and a young lady in a maroon two-piece will swoop down to help you, two-way radio at the ready. Platforms, times, connections at Luton, they can pluck the smallest detail out of the ether. This is the smiling face of customer care. No more timidly tapping a grumpy guard and risking rebuff, these girls can answer your questions before you've even thought of them.

A drawback to this guardian angel ploy is that it only works on willing victims, and when I see the hostess bearing down on a trainspotter I know there's going to be trouble.

'Can I help you, sir?' coos the young lady.

How sweet, but she might as well have been wielding a pickaxe on his pride. If there's anything trainspotters don't need it's guiding around the railway system. And being taken for a member of the public is even worse. Will he tell her to bugger off, or suffer her do-gooding with British fortitude?

'No thanks,' he says grumpily, jamming on his personal stereo headphones to emphasize his rebuff.

Smalltalk was always part of the pleasure of trainspotting, but it's not so easy now that many spotters are wired up to Sony Walkmans. We never had such luxury in the old days. If you were lucky you had a tinny transistor, if not you just had to hum to yourself. Not that I'd have turned my nose up at a Walkman, it's a lovely way to while away the gaps between the trains. But what exactly are they listening to? I wouldn't dare to generalize, but I do know that heavy metal is popular – Metallica, Anthrax, Aerosmith – music with a throb and a thrash that closely parallels the noise of diesels. If we analyzed it deeply enough I daresay we'd find identical wavelengths present in bass guitar riffs and Maybach engines.

031   The Care of Broccoli and Potato Traffic

I always make a point of going to the Burton Railway Club's annual fayre. The main attraction, for my children at least, are the model railways. Myself, I always suffer an ache of envy. I've always wanted a layout: a big one with a dozen trains, sidings full of weathered trucks, and old-fashioned signals that flip at the touch of a button. Unfortunately, I've never lived anywhere big enough to spare the room. There's the loft, but it would mean stripping out all that fluffy yellow insulation, and the house's heat would then float up to keep me warm, while the rest of the family might as well be sitting in a bus shelter. I couldn't do it to them. One day I will get round to having my own railway, but in the meantime I'm stuck with my envy.

At one of the layouts a blonde girl sits patiently while her boyfriend explains the finer points of his layout to the steady stream of spectators. I'm surprised that a trainspotter should have such a pretty girlfriend, then angry at myself for believing in stereotypes. In the end, I have to admit that it's sheer jealousy masquerading as surprise. Why shouldn't a girl love a man who loves small railways? It's a harmless pastime and displays feeling for old-fashioned community values, even if it is only in 00 gauge. Another odd notion this, that because a man has a hobby he's useless in bed and dull company. For all I know he may have the sexual dynamism of Tom Jones and a super sense of humour.

The big satisfaction of railway modelling is the chance to combine the roles of stationmaster, train driver and the Almighty (not that God ever took off his glasses and picked a sheep up with tweezers in order to give it a fresh lick of paint). These men in cardigans have spent so long on these layouts, they've created everything down to the washing on the line, the bicycle in the station yard and the porter with a barrowload of newspapers. But I doubt if anyone shares my slightly bizarre fantasy of being able to miniaturize myself and escape into the background of these imaginary market towns with contrived names: Woodbury Junction, Rudchester or Bellfordham. It would be a hell of a lark to grab a newspaper from the barrow and pedal off furiously on the little bicycle, flashing two fingers at the static constable with his old-fashioned helmet.

Elsewhere the stalls do their usual steady trade as punters flick through the neatly boxed paperwork. New books, musty books, picture books, technical books, leatherbound classics, flimsy leaflets, old timetables, Ian Allan *ABC*s, railway rule books; trainspotting has accumulated a staggering bibliography. It dates back well over a century and shows no sign whatsoever of dwindling. Between them, the railway companies and the hobbyists must have produced tens of thousands of books on trains, and even our local library has ten shelves full. With more gutsy ways of trainspotting dwindling,

233

the hobby shows signs of reverting to its old status as a scholarly subject. Those short-trousered boys of the 1930s are now active pensioners, with plenty of time for browsing, and the will to spend decent sums on sought-after books. They aren't trainspotters, since they have only disdain for the modern scene, but live firmly in the past, and now have the time to investigate the background, rummaging on the stalls not for simple picture books, but for learned and well-researched writing which binds up whole areas of history, sociology and economics with the railways.

I don't mind the picture books, but a lot of this stuff is way too arcane and specialized for me. I have absolutely no desire to buy or read *Fifty Years of Railway Signalling*, *Nineteenth-Century Railway Carriages* or *A Modeller's Guide to the LNER*. That said, some of these publications go so far past the edges of obscurity that they're too fascinating to resist. Like the Western Region's booklet instructing staff on *The Care of Broccoli and Potato Traffic* and the LMS' *Regulations for Railway Police* which warns 'on no account must females be handcuffed'. I forgive these books, they give railways a human edge.

I do love old timetables, though. They remind me of how I first began to discover the world, the joy of working out for myself how to get from Burton to Wolverhampton, and how to get back in time for tea. I copied the times out neatly in my notebook, and kept them close to me throughout the journey. There was always a nagging doubt as to whether these digits and details would really turn into solid trains. But when it all worked and I got to trust it, it gave me great confidence in the workings of society. We could do it, we could work together.

An old LMR timetable (£8.50) tempts me. Cynics might ask how a man can find anything to amuse him in a list of trains times, and ones from 1960 at that. But with these details we can close our eyes and travel again on the Euston–Carlisle express, dreaming ourselves through each stop. I can picture myself on some day in

1960: stopping at Lancaster station, waiting for the guard's green flag, watching the steam drift past the window, curling my toes in the heat from under the seats. I can live every minute of that imaginary journey, but not without the vital paperwork. The fun comes from knowing that the train did exist and that on one day, 17 January 1960, for instance, *Lovat Scout* or *Black Prince* took all those people to Carlisle. The driver and his fireman signed off and walked to the railway hostel for a bath and a meal. History comes alive through these pages.

Outside on the lawn, the local Model Engineering Society has set up a 30-yard length of track to run its loco on. The engine is a creation of love, and the driver, who wears a real cap of course, shovels the coal in with a dessert spoon. It's so English and comforting, and I can't understand why anyone should have a downer on men who like steam trains, big or small.

After an hour or so it's time to go, but first I have to promise an old spotting pal, Darb, who's manning the door, that I'll attend the next club night. I make the same promise every time I see him and, though time and commitments conspire against me, I always feel guilty about going there so rarely. This time I'm determined to keep my promise.

When I can get to a club night, I usually go with Jinx, but only if there's a proper film show with some real grimy steam in it. Neither of us has much time for the slide shows – the commentaries are invariably slow and self-indulgent, and the slides always have a knack of being put in upside down.

Darb mans the door here too, and takes my money promising to get me a pint in as a reward for keeping my word. I'm pleased to see him, but it's always hard to connect the grown man with a beard with the skinny beanpole you went to Crewe with. But most people who come here haven't lost touch with anyone. No one has turned tubby on them overnight. They went to junior school together, chased girls together and went to each other's weddings. The camaraderie is rock solid, and I envy them for that.

As well as being a club for trainspotters, the Railway Club also acts as reunion point for Burton's old steam men. These are the drivers and firemen who used to nod to us at Steamer Gates thirty years ago; the young married men with their lunchboxes and billycans. And now here they are again, in their Sunday-best ties and dentures. It's nice to know, though, that the boys at Steamer Gates got their wish in the end. If they were too late to be apprenticed as firemen, at least they can buy one of the old drivers a pint and sit down with them as equals.

Trainspotting is in danger of becoming part of the club-raffle culture, something to talk about between domino games and pints. We're not scruffs watching steamers any more, but for the price of a raffle ticket we stand a chance of winning a video of the Somerset and Dorset. When it's quiet you can hear the sipping of pints and scent the vaguely nostalgic smell of smoke from somebody's pipe.

All the same, I still have that uneasy feeling of not quite belonging. I love trains as much as the rest of the members (and besides, that love is not quantifiable), but I know my experience is different. It starts off the same, with the impressive Britannia, then the vaguely sci-fi electric. And the thrill must have been the same for all of us, whatever era we started in. But somewhere in the mid-seventies it went off on a tangent for me: the alienation of the China Clay Special, the lovely weekend in Fontainebleau, the reverse rebellion of travelling first class, the unbearable sadness of returning to old haunts, the smell of wormwood – to me all that is as much a part of the trainspotting scenario.

And then there's my mischievous wish to, at the same time as enjoying it all, look underneath and gently mock. Not about anoraks or neatly packed lunchboxes, but about the funny, infuriating, and baffling side of it all. I know I can't explain these things to anyone else at the Railway Club. I can make funny stories out of them for the entertainment of fellow drinkers, but that's not the real truth, just a polite way of fitting in. I just have to face the obvious truth: the railways have so many facets for me, I'm unable to enjoy my trainspotting with a clear conscience.

032   Freight's Great (Shame About the Wagons)

I've only taken my children spotting half a dozen times, but they're already bored with Sprinters and HSTs. I'm sorry, but there's not much magic to be found in railway stations nowadays. We have to face it, though; loco-hauled passenger trains are never going to come back into service, there'll be no more Britannias or Deltics blasting off under vaulted roofs, no more excited squeals at the noise, no running scared from the sudden belch of smoke. Those little dramas that made trainspotting such fun are getting harder to find.

If there's any drama and colour left, it has to be with freight trains.

For much too long, freight was the unsung hero of trainspotting. All the plaudits and the colour plates in boys annuals were reserved for the great expresses – The Pines, The Elizabethan, The Coronation Scot, The Cornish Riviera – the magnificent flyers the lads at the lineside longed to see. And all the while, in the background, were the goods trains, railway's ugly ducklings, getting on with life, keeping the country supplied with coal and butter and beer.

One good thing about privatization, from a spotter's point of view, is the return of the livery. The idea, old as history but still sound PR, has been taken up with gusto by the new freight companies Load Haul, Transrail and Mainline Freight. Some spotters were horrified when the colours were first unveiled. 'Garish! . . . vulgar! . . . inappropriate!' they yelled, and wrote to *RAIL* to say so. It was only to be expected after so many years of British Rail conformity. Liveries have always been emotive, which was one reason why BR did its utmost to get rid of them in the first place. But less conservative spotters loved the new look. Freight had suddenly got big and colourful. The PR departments and logo-makers had, unwittingly, put a bit of oomph back into the hobby. It's no wonder the spotters are flocking to places like Bescot, Toton and Tinsley.

The trainspotter's map of Britain is different to everyone else's. Names like Tinsley, Springs Branch, St Philip's Marsh and Stewarts Lane mean nothing to non-spotters. But these are nodal points on the railway network, the places where drivers clock on, diesels get fuelled up and trainspotters gather like moths round a candle. Toton's another prime location, a huge place with big zebra-striped doors and a yard full of diesels. As the only decent depot in the vicinity, it attracts plenty of trainspotters, even though it's in the middle of nowhere, a stiff windswept walk from Long Eaton station. On any day of the week, there's at least half a dozen of them hanging around, jotting down numbers or setting up tripods to photograph the assembled Egg-Timers and Class 60s.

Apart from an oil splash here and there and a driver's discarded *Sun*, its pages separating in the breeze, Toton, like all the other modern depots, is a remarkably clean place. From a distance the ballast looks as if it's been raked level by some lackey. The old elemental chaos has been eliminated; there's no untidiness, no junk, no piles of smouldering ash, no bent rakes, no tea emptied out in a sweeping splash. Even the engines, the Class 60s in particular, have such a clean profile they could have been drawn with the express purpose of illustrating a brochure. The bulbous noses and rattling ventilator grilles of the old diesels have been designed away. Today's engines have no superfluous bits, nothing to puzzle you, and nothing to fire the imagination. Still, they're not units, that's the main thing.

It must be ten years since I last bunked a depot, and I don't know if I still have the bottle. Back then it was a dare, a schoolboy escapade. But now . . . should I even be thinking of it? After all, I'd never dream of walking into a factory or a dairy or a fire station and looking around as if I owned the place. Whatever, no one would ever have suspected us of criminal trespass or industrial espionage, we were just kids trying it on. Today I have a curious child as an excuse if anyone says anything. But will our innocence and eccentricity still protect us?

It would be unreasonable of me to compare my sixties bunking with this unofficial visit to Toton, but I can't help wondering if the thrill is the same for those who do it today. We were high on the adrenalin thrill – but the trainspotters I've seen here today look casual and perfectly at ease. These aren't the kind of men who are going to risk tearing their trousers on a fence.

In the event, Robin and I walk around unhindered. Even when I trip over some fitter's pipeline he moves it out of the way for us, not with a curse but with an apology. Am I right then in thinking that an unofficial right of access is still recognized, that anyone with a genuine interest in trains is not turfed out like a hooligan? Or have we just been lucky? Perhaps it was always so. Meet the wrong employee on the wrong day and you got your backside kicked, go on another day and some kindly driver would happily take you for an unauthorized ride to the sidings and back.

Freight's great – dirty and noisy and gutsy – but it's thrown up an odd subculture in its wake. Wagonspotting. Railway magazines may have banned the word trainspotter, for now the mainstream part of the hobby comprises a lot more than noting numbers – taking photographs, chatting to railwaymen and fellow enthusiasts, soaking up the atmosphere. But a wagonspotter has to be just that – a spotter.

An engine was never inanimate. Steam or diesel, it had a character. It could be a noisy bad-tempered bugger, always letting its drivers down, or it could be as sweet as a nut, ever eager to please. It was as living an entity as could ever be made of steel and electric wiring. There was a loco, and there were carriages and wagons. You collected one and ignored the other. Wasn't that the cardinal rule hammered into me on that very first day in 1964? But with HSTs the lines began to get blurred. What were they exactly? Sleek locos of the future or just glorified bog units? Was the bit at the front a locomotive, or just a carriage with an engine? But surely no one can deny that a wagon is an inanimate object. It doesn't have one jot of charisma. There are no heroics involved. Wagonspotting entails lonely visits to soulless depots, walking along long lines of identical coal trucks and mineral hoppers. Still, the point is, every wagon has a number. And that's enough for some people.

They even have their own regular wagonspotters column, wittingly entitled 'Wagons Roll', in *RAIL* magazine. This is spotting at its worst and dullest extreme. It may be news that two men drove a diesel from A to B, it has a human angle, but the fact that VDA van BDC210323 has gone into Doncaster Works for repair and a new grey and yellow livery is a fact of supreme uninterest. Except to wagonspotters, I suppose. It might be tempting to mock the concerns and jargon of wagonspotters – why was an MKA, in reality a privately owned PGA hopper, disguised as a ZKA?, and what on earth is a Coalfish? – but that kind of cheap pseudo-analysis could be used to look at any hobby. In any case, I just don't want to know the answers. There's a very real danger of being attracted to the very thing you mock, just as those who deride TV soaps end up not bearing to miss an episode.

There's a wagon depot here in Burton, and I've seen these sad souls myself, walking the gullies between the wagons, jotting down the number of every coal truck and mineral hopper. Some of them mumble into dictaphones and sort it all out later. I feel sorry for them, for I can well understand it for what it is: a sad attempt to recreate the awesome challenge that trainspotting once was. With so many carriages scattered around the country, tracking them all down will fill in a good twenty years or so.

The thing is, no one really, not in their hearts, wants to finish. You spot for years to finish off a class, and completing one class is all right. But once you have all of them, a frightening emptiness comes yawning up. In the fifties there were upwards of 18,000 train numbers for a lad to collect – a lifetime's quest. By 1968, 16,000 of them had been struck from the books. But the glee of diesel-lovers was short-lived. Ten years later their Peaks and Deltics and Warships were off to the scrapyard too. Today's spotters, with the dosh and mobility we could only dream of, can see the thousand or so locos in a couple of years. So some new challenge is imperative. The number-crunching addiction must be fed.

Once you blur these lines, where does it stop? The answer is that it doesn't, and it exposes the dottiness within. It was OK for kids to collect the numbers of steam engines, but you can't blame people for thinking the worst of a man who collects the numbers of wagons. And there's worse. I know of spotters who set out to have a cup of tea in every station buffet on BR, or bashers whose only ambition is to clock up 500 miles behind every Class 87 electric. Any excuse will do to get on those trains and head off up the line. I've even heard of people who collect the serial numbers of the chocolate machines on the London Underground. Serious madness, perhaps, but beyond the scope of this book.

033 Je Suis un Trainspotter Anglais

The *chef de la gare* is furious. The platforms at Agde are unusually lengthy, and having walked them in the skin-sizzling sun to investigate the two bodies reported by an anxious passenger, he's flabbergasted to find two British trainspotters, one dozing, the other stretched out reading an old *Daily Mail*. Blissfully unaware of the stir they've caused, Jim tries to engage *le chef* with a bit of schoolboy French, starting off with the obvious '*Il fait très chaud!*' and moving on to an ambitious, clumsily phrased question about whether there'll be a Class 7100 electric on the next motorail train from Spain.

The station master, younger than his British counter-part and quite hip in mirrored shades and a crisp blue shirt, mutters a string of expletives and turns his back on them to start the long trudge back to the cool of his office. He looks as if he might ring his colleagues further down the line and warn them there's some English loon-ies on the loose.

Trainspotters from Britain are an increasingly common sight in Europe. Self-conscious at home, ever on the look-out for smirks and unkind remarks, they've decided to take their custom elsewhere. And, of course, there's the fact that British Rail is getting too boring these days. For those not willing to bite the bullet and take up wagonspotting (and some would rather have a British wagon than a foreign diesel any day) there's the prospect of crossing the Channel and starting again from scratch. Now the Channel Tunnel is open, the temp-tation is hard to resist. It means faster times, and no more wasted hours on ferries and connecting buses. From Doncaster to Dijon they are cosseted in their very own culture.

Jim and Chris have stopped off at Agde after an

unofficial visit to the loco works at Béziers, just down the line. They've had a good day so far and underlined a couple of dozen numbers in their spotting books (French locos but a British book). Now they're hoping to get some good shots of trains speeding up country towards Marseille and Lyon. When the traffic eases off a bit, they might give the station a miss for a couple of hours and pop down to that naturist beach they've read about.

It's tempting to imagine these Eurospotters as wandering philistines, impervious to the charms of local life. Not a bit of it. Though they tend to stick to fast food (Hot Dog's the same in any language), Jim and Chris can recognize a good salad niçoise when they see one. There's also a grudging respect for the local beer, which looks as pale as piss, but is a great knock-out to ease the discomfort of kipping on the overnight trains. There is scope for schoolboy jokes and mildly xenophobic mockery, yet, although it would be a brilliant wind-up after their experience earlier in the day, neither of them dares ask Agde's *chef de la gare* if he's the man in charge of the refreshment room.

Trainspotting has always been a peculiarly British hobby, though no one has ever known exactly why. My own theory is that it was all tied up with patriotism and loyalty and Empire. It was propaganda on wheels. We had an endless list of writers and admirals and victories to celebrate, hundreds of stately homes and colonies, and when steam was gone the notion was simply transferred to the diesels.

But an interest in railways is not unknown abroad: there are steam buffs as far away as Canada and Australia; model railway clubs are quite popular in Denmark, Switzerland and Germany; and Frenchmen still take their children to see the Chapelon pacifics at the railway museum in Mulhouse. But despite such widespread enthusiasm for railways it's only the British (in Europe at any rate) who have nurtured a fascination for collecting train and wagon numbers.

Browsing through the *European Loco Pocket Book* for France, the official numbering systems seem anodyne and the classes have little in the way of character. The B63400 class is followed by the B63500 class, the Y5100 by the Y6200s. There are no equivalent to Peaks or Warships or Deltics, though I suspect the railwaymen must have their own nicknames. This is in sharp contrast to Britain. I wonder if the hobby would ever have had the same appeal had it been purely numerical, if there'd been no Castles or Scots or the rest of them. Is it chauvinistic to think of British trains as more colourful? Or is it part of the trainspotter's agenda to impose that colour on top of everything? At the end of the day, without the trainspotter to put it all in relief and write a mythology, the railways – British, French or Indian – are just a transport system, more or less efficient, and largely taken for granted. As Eurospotting spreads, so will the nick-naming and the spoken tales.

Things have changed a lot since I first travelled to France, shivering my way to Paris on that dull green train in 1975. The French have arguably the best rail network in Europe. Even the most chauvinistic of trainspotters can be heard praising the SNCF to the skies.

On the 10.10 TGV from Gare de Lyon to Montpellier, Dave jabs the button of his stopwatch. 'Valence–Montélimar, 22 minutes, 12 seconds.' He does a few quick scribbles on his notepad and whistles. 'Hellfire!'

He is won over, an instant convert to the TGV. His friend Pete is less sure and leaps to the defence of Britain's East Coast timetable. There follows a ping-pong match of statistics, which passes another ten minutes, until the third member of their party returns from the buffet with a can of Coke and a sandwich that looks like a small log.

'Four bloody quid!' he seethes, much to their merriment as they tuck into the Walkers crisps and lukewarm Fanta they've been carrying since they left the Midlands the day before.

The style of European trains puts bashers reluctantly on their best behaviour. Back home they'd be wandering up and down, sticking their heads out of the window to catch numbers in passing yards. European trains tend to have hydraulic doors and unopenable windows, a much safer practice, but one that's not appreciated by bashers who like to feel the wind in their hair.

Modernization always has its price. What I hate most about the TGV are all the rows of seats facing the same way. It makes spontaneous friendships and inter-station flirtations sadly rare. (At least Britain has stuck largely to its four-seats-and-a-table arrangement, and I think BR deserve credit for this.) But there's one thing Europe does have, one last fling of romanticism and adventure in the trainspotter's life. Overnight trains. Hundreds of them. The whole of Europe slows right down after midnight and you can snooze the night away on dusty seats between Bordeaux and Marseille, Lisbon and Porto Campanhã or Prague and Zilina.

As yet, the trainspotter is still an enigma, left to pursue his quest in peace. They come in well-mannered groups of two or three at a time, booking into modest hotels and generally keeping themselves to themselves. Though isolated outbreaks of rowdiness have been reported in Britain, Europe has yet no reason to fear an annual invasion of trainspotters as it does football fans. But who knows . . .

It's not just France that attracts the Eurospotter. Germany and the Netherlands are popular destinations too. And with spotting books available for countries as far-flung as Portugal, Norway and Finland, you can be sure that if there's a list of locos there'll be someone who wants to tick them all off with green ink. And there'll always be one snob who likes to think himself one step ahead, and so when France becomes even more popular he will be bashing the 1800 Co-Cos in Portugal.

Few Eurospotters have more than a smattering of the local lingo. But the language of railways is an unspoken one. Just as it needs no linguistic skills to appreciate the cathedrals of Cologne and Rouen, so it takes the train buff no time to orientate himself on the railway bridges and platforms of Antwerp, Hamburg and Lyon. He has a sixth sense, honed by years of studying manuals and books. Like Superman with his X-ray vision, it takes only a brief stare at some enigmatic lineside box before he has a convincing explanation of its workings and its function in the railway system.

While many Eurospotters relish the challenges, some, like Tony from Derby, wander around looking for echoes of the past. He still misses his summer days at Plymouth and Exeter, and the distinctive roar of the Western's Warships. When they were scrapped in the 1970s he went off to Northern Germany in pursuit of the V200s, a loco on which the Warships themselves were originally based. Reliving the past became easy. When they too were withdrawn, he was quite disconsolate. Until he read that the Germans had sold off a batch of the V200s to the Greeks. Now he's planning a trip to Athens to get a few more snaps for his archives.

Tony's lucky. Like many of his fellow enthusiasts he's a BR employee and, with concessionary fares, can travel the length and breadth of Europe virtually for free. For others Eurospotting can be cripplingly expensive. But Jim and Chris have got a brilliant master-plan to head off complaints about the drain on the family budgets. They're going to break with the Paignton routine next year and bring their wives and kids down to Langue-doc. Again, it's a perfect arrangement. The kids get a Mediterranean holiday, Jim and Chris can swan off to Avignon to notch up some BB 9400s, and the lot of them can all go home with a tan to show off to the neighbours.

After Europe? Well, there's always America. They can't go there by train, of course, but the USA is the one place where they'll find anything like a trainspotting culture.

I don't know if they collect numbers, but they certainly love their trains. And, being the Big Country, it's not surprising that they do things in a big way. They've got the Casey Jones hats, of course, and replica lamps from the Rock Island Line. All quite normal, really. But where else would you get a telephone that alerts you with the sound of a steamer blowing its whistle? And would Barclays ever offer to overprint your cheques with full-colour steamer locos from the Santa Fe or the Illinois Central?

British enthusiasts buy videos and books about the Illinois Central and the Rock Island Line, yet this trade is nearly all one-way. Americans aren't interested in books about the Somerset and Dorset or videos about the Doncaster Works Open Day. It smacks of the old one-sided arrangement we've put up with ever since the nylons and chewing gum years.

And where's our runaway train coming down the track? Mind you, our trains have never been chased by irritated Sioux or blasted to matchsticks by bandits with dynamite. Maybe that's why, despite the violence, the Great Train Robbery is still cherished, our one moment of Wild West adventure, misted by history, blurred through the veil of a Woolworths stocking.

What's more, the Americans actually sing about their trains. They ain't self-conscious, no sir! And here's the three-volume boxed set to prove it, with Johnny Cash and Boxcar Willie belting out 'Night Train to Memphis', 'Freight Train Blues', 'Daddy was a Railroad Man', and 'Blow that Lonesome Whistle'. How can we match such redneck enthusiasm? Why, if trainspotting is so British, has there never been a songbook to match? Where are all the songs about the midnight sleeper to Penzance or a long, clanking train of mineral hoppers? Even when railways were mentioned in those British pop songs of the sixties there were never any details, we were too polite to talk about rust and grease and filthy smoke. The Americans positively revelled in their traditions: the railways were still part of the Wild West and every boxcar-hopping hobo had a tale composed of equal measures of grit and melancholy.

If I could play the mouth organ, I'd go down on the platform at Burton-on-Trent and compose myself a lonely blues. It's time trainspotting came up with some home-grown standards.

> I went down to Burton station (ooh-wah)
> I didn't see no more steamers up the line
> Them Jubes and them Jinties is all gone now
> I'm just a-sitting here cryin'.

> Let me tell ya it's all Sprinters now (ooh-wah)
> There ain't no romance any more
> There ain't no smoke on the 'rizon
> The whole damned scene's got such a bore.

Postscript: Burton-on-Trent, 1995

Watching Robin with his first trainspotting book, I'm as excited as he is. I can feel myself clutching it, fascinated by the glossy pages, the vaporous smell and the long columns of numbers. Like me in 1964, he's not sure of the difference between one loco and another or which number you write down, but he's a quick learner. In time he'll have the jargon off pat.

An Egg-Timer comes blasting out from under the railway bridge taking a long, rattling line of coal wagons out to the power station. Robin used to be scared, but now he loves the thunder. What child wouldn't? I'm amused. How could I have dreamt that one day, long years after the Duck Sixes and Ozzies at Steamer Gates, I'd be standing here admiring an Egg-Timer?

After School. Oliver and Robin, my children, wave as a veteran Class 37 rumbles through Burton Station with a train of flat wagons, March 1995

Burton station is hardly the most exciting venue these days, but we don't have much choice. Most of the old spotting places have been demolished or made inaccessible – a boxing club now stands on the site of Little Burton Bridges, and the grass where we used to sprawl by Steamer Gates is now a Toyota garage. The biggest loss of all, for me anyway, was the footbridge at Wetmore Sidings. It was in the way of 'development', so they sold what they could as scrap metal and burnt the rest. All those boards etched with train numbers and the autographs of Gaz, Kev and Duggy, they all went up in smoke. Just down the road from Wetmore, my friends Janice and Ian live in a small terrace of starter homes built across the site of Horninglow station. They don't even remember the caff, let alone the station, yet the railway runs under their house like some pagan ley line. I wonder whether the clack of wheels and the slam of carriage doors echoes in their dreams some nights.

No one would have taken any notice of trainspotters in days gone by. They were part of the railway scenery like porters or pigeon baskets. Now they stand out like a sore thumb, viewed with suspicion and amusement. The office girls waiting for their trains stare open-mouthed and stand back as a trainspotter passes. They exchange smirks; thank God none of them has a trainspotter for a fella. Strangely enough, they don't even notice Robin and me. There's nothing at all wrong in a man taking his young son to watch the trains.

In the fifties and sixties trainspotting was real *Beano*-type fun, The Bash Street Kids versus British Rail, with grumpy porters and stationmasters kicking schoolboy ass. These days, though, the relationship is much cosier. Ever since British Railways took up advertising in *ABC* spotting books (£350 p.a. for a boy of 16 in 1962) the railways have been staffed by fifth columnists enjoying travel concessions, and welcoming fellow bashers with open arms. Nose around any modest-sized station and the odds are you'll find the chargeman's office doubles as a bashers' club, a place where shivering spotters can get warm and catch up on the latest info. And no matter if there's no buffet, the chargeman will do a brew when he's finished his platform announcements (that background crackle you hear isn't faulty electrics, it's just a basher diving into a packet of smoky bacon crisps).

The old gang are still around, though none of us does any serious spotting now. Andy is News Editor on the local paper and sticks old train pictures in whenever he finds an excuse. Since a kind aunt bought him a pair of binoculars one Christmas he's been heavily into bird-watching. I wouldn't compare it with trainspotting, but it gets you out into the fresh air and, even better, unlike trainspotting, it's refreshingly free of heartbreak.

Pipsqueak, under his proper name of course, became a regular writer to the letters page of the *Burton Mail*. One letter was about his encounter with a blind trainspotter at Steamer Gates who could identify the trains by their sounds and smells. Even for him it was a bit bizarre. But one day I heard two old women talking on the bus about 'that mad bloke who writes them silly letters to the paper', and I felt insulted on Pipsqueak's behalf. So what if I thought the letter a laugh, I admired whatever he was trying to say about our lack of imagination, the kind of life that's available to us and our kids since the end of steam.

And me, I've written this book. I thought I started it in 1994, but I think I really began writing it one day in 1964.

Nostalgia is a badly abused word these days, embracing everything from tatty horse-brasses to ploughman's lunches. Pure whimsy. Real nostalgia is a sickness. I've had it sometimes, when things weren't so good – a really desperate desire to go back, to be that kid again. Not just for the steam engines and the rattling wagons in the sidings, but for the certainties which only the past can offer: the certainty that you can go home, that Mum will do you a quick beans-on-toast if you're hungry, that there'll be a lovely fire you can sit in front of and mark off your cops, that *Z-Cars* will be on the telly. Smells are the fatal triggers: the sulphurous whiff I sometimes get from our coal fire, the tang of diesel perhaps, or, especially, the dry fragrance of wormwood. Wormwood is a bluey-green herb that sprouts up in any old grotty patch. There was tons of it at Wetmore Sidings. A while back I actually bought some from a garden centre to plant in our back garden. In summer, when the fragrance reaches me, I can close my eyes, and the nostalgia for Wetmore Sidings hurts: the pictures are so sharp, the pain so dull and endless. It's the past yet again. All the time, the past. No one dares look too far into the future; they're scared it has no smell. In the world of electromagnetic levitation there'll be no tang of diesel fuel, no bitter whiff of brake dust, and no flowers between the tracks. We know it full well, but we're scared to put it into words. That fearful future without hobbies or humour or secret hiding places. Where our children are wired up like smoking beagles.

I can't help wondering if I would ever have started trainspotting if it hadn't been for Bolt. How easily that moment could have slipped away from me, a childish offer, so easily rejected. Yet I can't imagine my life without the railways in it. Would I still have travelled to all those places, and even if I had, wouldn't I have gone by aeroplane? The railways kept me down to earth and prevented me getting smugly private and worrying about my status. Is it too fanciful to think that the railways helped make me into a democrat?

As I got closer to finishing the book, hoping I'd covered all angles, there was yet another derogatory reference to trainspotters. This time on Radio Two: a *Guardian* journalist filling in with a comic turn between pop records. Out come all the usual props and the same complaints. The joke is long past its sell-by date, yet media folk still rely on it for an easy laugh.

In fact the media claim to have science on their side now that some boffin has identified trainspotters as suffering from Asperger's Syndrome – a pathological compulsion to control and order the outside world. Is there any human being who doesn't have some urge to make sense of their world, to enjoy it in the open air and learn about its ways, and cohabit with it to the best of his or her enjoyment? Of course not. To suggest that trainspotters have taken a simple caprice and turned it into a pathological disorder is plainly nonsense.

One of the oddest things is the belief that trainspotters spend all their time trainspotting, as though it isn't just a weekend thing or a holiday thing. None of them would believe that a scuba-diver is a scuba-diver while he's at the office or that a football fan goes to a disco in his kit. So why do they believe that trainspotting is a permanent state of being?

Was it Jasper Carrott who started it all? Some trainspotters think he's got a lot to answer for, but I can forgive him (just), since in a democratic society everyone should take their turn as an Aunt Sally. It's flattering to be lampooned, and even trainspotters can laugh at themselves. What is unforgivable is the way the media have hijacked a joke and turned it into received wisdom. And what is frightening is how they've abused the trust of their readers. People are now convinced that trainspotters, even if they don't know one, are boring, clueless and sexless.

The same old jokes. But after I'd finished yawning, I got to thinking, what the hell is it about trainspotters that they are so frightened of? What syndrome do such people suffer from who can worry and gnaw at the same meatless bone for years on end, deluded and angry, convinced that there is meat on it when there isn't? It's a kind of fetishism, really. These detractors have got the anorak to get them going, but their obsession blinds them to the fact that that's all it is, a coat with a zip. Like all fetishists, just like those men who steal women's knickers from washing-lines, they desperately want the clothing to contain the object of desire. But there is no nerd with glasses or puddingbowl haircut or four different-coloured biros. The anorak is empty.

'Get a life, get a life' is their constant admonition. But what *life* exactly are they talking about? What constitutes excitement in this leisure-based society? Watching *Match of the Day*? Shopping at B&Q? Visiting McDonald's? I'm constantly on the lookout these days for cheery faces bursting with *joie de vivre*. I want to ask them their secret of a full life. But I've yet to come across anyone who fits that description. Everyone I see seems satisfied with the video from the corner shop, the Berni-Inn meal, getting hopelessly pissed on a Friday, fighting for a parking space on Saturday, sleeping off Sunday. Where is this life? On all the evidence trainspotting is one of the few pastimes that engages people in the general hum of society, that throws people together in a hurly-burly way to talk and watch and have a laugh and soak up a bit of history.

Back at Burton, the sun has come out, the signals are green and the 125 is off on its way to Paignton. We watch it go. I wish we were on it, but the thrill of watching other people depart is always a compensation.

This is trainspotting – the next generation. But I'm wary of setting up my children as figures of fun. It doesn't seem as if the public will ever shake this stereotyped trainspotter from their vocabulary. When breakfast TV host Richard Madeley got an insulting hoax phone call he immediately drew an analogy with trainspotting. 'These are sad people. These are anoraks. It's so easy to get a hoax on television. It's like a train thing to do. Go and spot some trains or buy yourself an anorak, love.'

Is this how they'll treat my children if they carry on liking trains? If that's the case I ought to drop the idea straight away, go back to basics, like magnetism and Lego Technik. But why should we live our lives according to the diktats of the (supposedly) fashionable agenda-setters? I'd rather see trainspotting as a more useful lesson, an introduction to a world of trains and passengers and railwaymen and women, a communal enterprise. Certainly my suspicion of cars comes into it. I don't want my boys to live the rest of their lives travelling in a metal box, seeing nothing, speeding by, tensed up over a wheel, trying to show off, or becoming one of the people killed on the roads each year. Trainspotting is just the start, the first step on that InterRail journey round Europe. I'm not wishing their lives away, but I can't wait to see my sons setting off with their rucksacks and girlfriends, arm-in-arm.

As for me, I couldn't give a cuss what anyone else thinks about trainspotting. *Je ne regrette rien.* Some people might say it's been a monumental waste of thirty years, but I just can't agree.

Out of the blue...

*IND*IGO

the best in modern writing

FICTION

Nick Hornby *High Fidelity*	£5.99	0 575 40018 8
Kurt Vonnegut *The Sirens of Titan*	£5.99	0 575 40023 4
Joan Aiken *Mansfield Revisited*	£5.99	0 575 40024 2
Daniel Keyes *Flowers for Algernon*	£5.99	0 575 40020 x
Joe R. Lansdale *Mucho Mojo*	£5.99	0 575 40001 3
Stephen Amidon *The Primitive*	£5.99	0 575 40017 x
Julian Rathbone *Intimacy*	£5.99	0 575 40019 6
Janet Burroway *Cutting Stone*	£6.99	0 575 40021 8

NON-FICTION

Gary Paulsen *Winterdance*	£5.99	0 575 40008 0
Robert K. Massie *Nicholas and Alexandra*	£7.99	0 575 40006 4
Hank Wangford *Lost Cowboys*	£6.99	0 575 40003 x
Biruté M. F. Galdikas *Reflections of Eden*	£7.99	0 575 40002 1
Stuart Nicholson *Billie Holiday*	£7.99	0 575 40016 1
Giles Whittell *Extreme Continental*	£6.99	0 575 40007 2

*IND*IGO books are available from all good bookshops or from:

> Cassell C.S.
> Book Service By Post
> PO Box 29, Douglas I-O-M
> IM99 1BQ
> telephone: 01624 675137, fax: 01624 670923

While every effort is made to keep prices steady, it is sometimes necessary to increase prices at short notice. Cassell plc reserves the right to show on covers and charge new retail prices which may differ from those advertised in the text or elsewhere.